Human
CAPABILITY

A Study of Individual Potential and its Application

Human
CAPABILITY

A Study of Individual Potential and its Application

JAQUES & CASON

Cason Hall *&* Co. Publishers
Falls Church, VA

Copyright © 1994 Elliott Jaques and Kathryn Cason
Potential Progress Data Sheet and Time Horizon Chart © Elliott Jaques, 1963, 1990

First published 1994

Cason Hall & Co. Publishers Ltd.
5201 Leesburg Pike
Suite 1103
Falls Church, VA 22041
Editorial Offices: 703-820-6200

ISBN 0-9621070-7-7

A CIP catalog record for this book is available from the Library of Congress.

∞ The paper used in this publication meets the minimum requirements of the American National
Standard for Information Sciences—Permanence of Paper for Printed Library Materials, ANSI Z39,
48-1984

Typeset in 11 on 13 Garamond
by Right Angle Graphics

Printed in the United States of America by
RR Donnelley & Sons Company

To Roland Gibson
and
John Isaac

Contents

Illustrations

Preface

A Question of Ethics

The authors were faced with a seemingly difficult ethical dilemma in approaching the research reported herein and in deciding to publish the results of that research. The dilemma has to do with the nature of the possible impact upon society of providing it with a form of knowledge that would make it possible *as a matter of ordinary everyday observation over a period of time* for people not only to evaluate their own and others' current level of potential capability, but also to articulate those judgments in a way readily understandable by others. To understand this dilemma, picture a situation in which parents could make an accurate evaluation of the level of potential capability of their children; teachers of their pupils—and young adult students of their teachers; friends of each other; spouses of each other; and on and on to everyone of everyone.

To illustrate further, imagine a nation in which all citizens were able, given enough encounters, to evaluate the level of potential capability of each and every one of the candidates running for election in political campaigns, by observing certain manifest features of their performances when engaged in spontaneous political debate, as, for example, on television. And "evaluate" is used here in the sense of being able to articulate that evaluation in a form that could be understood by others, so that the innate capability of their candidates could become a matter of everyday discussion and consideration. It is true, of course, that we all do now make such judgments of each other. But we cannot do so in a confident way. Nor are we able to articulate these judgments in a manner that can be meaningfully shared with others in accord with some common concepts and language for doing so. For up until now, with one exception, no such concepts and language have existed. The exception is that of work that has been carried out in the course of developments in creating requisite organizations.[1] It has to do with a talent pool mapping procedure in which managers-once-removed are provided with procedures for evaluating the potential capability of subordinates-once-removed in terms of their judged potential to work at particular organizational layers.[2] A systematic procedure for cross-checking and follow-up is included, as described in chapter 8, but the point here is that all of us do make these judgments, and under proper conditions can do so accurately. The research to be reported strongly supports this view. But it is a different matter to make a systematic set of concepts and language openly available to everyone under any and all conditions, and that was our concern. We would emphasize, however, as stated in chapter 8, that we retain the talent pool mapping procedure for evaluations within employment organizations, in order to preserve and enhance the very important mentoring and career development accountabilities of managers towards their subordinates-once-removed.[3]

To sharpen the issue, we had reason to believe when we started the research that if our hypotheses were supported, we would likely end up with precisely the consequences described. As we will report, the hypotheses have been supported by the research. If our findings are supported by further studies, then we will have placed into society a body of knowledge that will bring into being a sharp change in the way people know each other. The knowledge to which we refer, that of potential capability, is that of the highest level at which a person could currently work, in work that the person really valued doing, and for which he or she had had the opportunity to gain the necessary experience and skilled knowledge. It is what is variously referred to as a person's innate capability, or intelligence, or mental capacity, or raw native ability, or what we strive to measure (but fail) by IQ or other similar so-called mental tests.

---

1. Described in Jaques (1989) *Requisite Organization*, Cason Hall & Co. The glossary in *Requisite Organization* is the foundation for the glossary in this book.
2. Described in Jaques and Clement (1991) *Executive Leadership*. See especially the final chapter.
3. *ibid.*

Jaques & Cason

For us to know each other's potential capability accurately and explicitly would change things in many ways, for size of potential capability does have a substantial effect upon the quality of our interpersonal and working relationships—in work, in families, in politics, and in every other kind of social circumstance. Our assumptions and judgments about potential capability influence our choice of partners in work and in marriage, our choice of friends, political voting, our selection of employees and appointment of subordinates, our choice of university entrants. And failure to make good judgments is exceedingly costly—rejecting people unfairly, placing them in positions they do not have the potential capability to fill (an especially painful situation in many family businesses), electing politicians who are not up to handling the complexity of their positions (an especially painful situation in many governments), or negatively prejudiced underrecognition of the potential capability of individuals because of gender, color, minority group background, race, education, age, or religion, or even of physical handicap.

The fact is that we make judgments of the potential capability of individuals all the time, under circumstances where it matters in no uncertain fashion both for the individuals and for the institutions or social relationships in which they are involved. So long as there is no objective, openly available, and socially shareable method of evaluating potential capability, and of stating it in a commonly understandable language, serious mistakes can be made and are made. But even worse, and here is the nub of the matter from the ethical point of view, judgments of this most important quality of a person can be readily distorted by narrow prejudice reflecting unfair biases of many kinds.

Given the biases and stereotypes of our society, it is easy to underestimate the true potential capability of women, of African-Americans, of non-acculturated immigrant groups, of high capability graduates because "they are too young," or of individuals over sixty because "they are too old." It is equally easy to overestimate the potential capability of those who fit the majority mold, be it that of WASP, or MBA, or old-boy network, or even members of one's own minority group, and so over-promote or otherwise overrecognize the wrong persons to the detriment and damage of everyone—from strained families, to the undermining of our national business competitiveness when such judgments lead to incompetence at the top.

Jaques & Cason

Our clear and explicit judgment, therefore, has been that to be able to develop an objective, openly available, socially shareable method of evaluating and stating individual potential capability, and one that is both *reliable* and *valid,* is to be unequivocally on the side of the social good from the ethical point of view. If the innate potential capability of women, African-Americans, racial and ethnic minorities, those from the ghettoes, or the educationally deprived, could be made transparently clear to all, then the possibilities of deprivation based upon bias and prejudice would be markedly reduced—and that would be a significant ethical gain. It is but one more example of the fact that valid knowledge is on the side of the good—and that it is ignorance that supports prejudice and evil. Thus it is that we decided to get on with our work with the greatest dispatch.

We have encountered another criticism couched in ethical terms about which the critics have powerfully strong feelings. That criticism is to the effect that it is fundamentally wrong to pigeonhole or label people as having this or that level of potential capability. It is held to be degrading, or diminishing, or derogatory to suggest that someone had the potential capability to work "only" at, say, shop floor level, or "merely" as a tradesperson or clerk or a junior supervisor and so on.

This type of criticism is based upon covert arrogance. It assumes that no one at a lower level of innate potential than oneself could possibly be satisfied to be there. Those people who hold such an outlook seem to be unaware that it would imply that others of still higher capability than themselves must in turn have such a derogatory attitude toward them. This attitude is further reinforced by the view, particularly prevalent in the United States, that no self-respecting person could possibly be satisfied with anything less than a continuous aspiration to get to the very top, whatever that might be, and is driven by dissatisfaction with anything less.

This view of human nature is seriously incorrect. As our study clearly confirms, people seek, in the very deepest sense, to be recognized and appreciated for what they really are—neither more nor less. That is the real meaning of valuing the individual. And if there is one thing that each of us is crystal clear about, despite popular belief to the contrary, it is our innate potential capability. And that is the capability we seek the opportunity to exercise—not some will-o'-the-wisp which someone else thinks we ought to chase.

Jaques & Cason

To the extent, then, that our findings contribute to the possibility that individual capability can be recognized and accurately evaluated in a socially shareable form, this research will have made a contribution to strengthening the process of valuing ourselves and others for what we are as social beings and not as being better or worse because of differences in innate capability. Such a contribution has, in our view, a strong positive moral and ethical connotation.

Finally, we would point out that our findings have to do not with a static conception of human capability, but with a dynamic conception of the maturation of potential from infancy to old age. We shall return to this question of ethics in chapter 7 when we consider our findings from this current study in relation to other findings about maturation and growth potential and questions about predestination.

In sum, then, we believe that our findings can make a sound and constructive contribution to those with a genuine concern for improving the efficacy of our social institutions. And we feel sure that they can contribute to the well-being of individuals by helping both to deepen our understanding of our own true potential and to obtain the fair and just treatment that would bestow upon us that greatest gift of all: the opportunity to use our potential to the fullest. Therein lies true social morality.

Acknowledgements

We wish to thank each and every one of the individuals who participated as subjects in this study. We are grateful for the trust they placed in our ability to maintain confidence with respect to the personal views they shared with us, that enabled them in turn to provide us with the rich supply of information that has given us our results.

Alec Smith, Chairman and CEO, Gilbert Associates, Reading PA, and Jack Brady, Group Executive, Human Resources, and his colleagues at CRA, Melbourne, Australia, agreed to the study and set up all the conditions that made it possible. Without their active support and collaboration there would have been no project.

Dr. T. Owen Jacobs, of the US Army Research Institute for the Social and Behavioral Sciences, gave strong technical support for the design of the research and the analysis of the data, and provided supporting data. Dr. Phil Lewis, Professor of Psychology at Auburn University, enhanced many of these technical discussions. Dr. Jerry Harvey, Professor of Organization Development at George Washington University, helped with a meticulous and detailed critique of the manuscript, as did Dr. Harry Levinson of the Levinson Institute. Dr. Herb Koplowitz was of inestimable help in creative work on the connections between the four types of mental processes and Piaget's developmental stages, and other systems, such as symbolic logic and numbers scaling.

Nancy Lee assisted by taking part in the subsidiary study of how readily the method of identifying the various types of mental processing can be learned and in final editing of the manuscript.

Rebecca Cason's many talents, in-depth knowledge of the technical material and publishing expertise, enabled her to make significant contributions to every aspect of the preparation of the book, ranging from critique of the content of the manuscript, to page layout and illustration for the cover.

Mary Preston, of The Big Idea, designed the cover. Carol Sorgen copyedited the manuscript. Gary Roush did the typesetting. Rhoda Fowler typed the transcripts of the interview material and prepared the index. Nancy Kiser typed the manuscript. Olga Mulcahy prepared the chart for the maturation of complexity of mental processing from infancy to old age and did much final typing. Michelle Martch assisted in the final editing.

We are especially grateful to Robyn Budd for her dedication and support, and for coordinating the whole production process, from innumerable draft manuscripts through final printing and binding.

We have dedicated the book to our two friends and colleagues, John Isaac and Roland Gibson, who, before they retired, were affiliated with Brunel University. They have done outstanding work in linking, on the one hand, discontinuity theory, sentential logical processes, levels and connections, and truth table logic with, on the other hand, a foundation for the understanding of mental processes. Anyone who wished to test the validity of this judgment can do so by reference to their writings in the book *Levels of Abstraction in Logic and Human Action*.[1] The lack of recognition for their intellectual creativity stems from the fact, unfortunately, that most psychologists will have difficulty with their logical and mathematical models, and few logicians will appreciate the linking of these models to human thought. Were that George Boole was still with us!

---

1. Jaques, Gibson, and Isaac (1978).

Jaques & Cason

PART I

Basic Concepts

1

Human Capability and Work

One of the most important of human capabilities is the capability to work. Whether or not it is more or less important than the capability to procreate is a moot point which need not bother us here. Work and procreation are both so absolutely essential for the survival and adaptation of the human species that it would be a fruitless exercise to try to rank-order them. For it is through our work that we produce the necessities of life, maintain our political and governmental systems and services, run our homes and care for our families, teach our children, care for the ill, create works of art, and even carry out our recreational activities.

Yet, despite its critical importance, very little is known about work: it does not have a straightforward and generally accepted definition and meaning (even among work-study specialists and among so-called experts in the organization and management of work systems). And our lack of knowledge about work is compounded by our lack of knowledge about the meaning of the capability to be able to do it.

What we do know, in very general terms, is that some people are able to do something that might be called "higher levels of work" than others, variously referred to as more "highly responsible" work, or "bigger jobs," or more "complex" work, or more "difficult" work: not just more work in quantity, but somehow greater or lesser in scope or degree. But this peculiar quality of greater and lesser (or higher and lower) capability in work has never been measured.

Approximations to such measurement have been attempted in various types of intelligence testing. But there is no more adequate definition

3

of intelligence than there is of work, and intelligence tests have been validated mainly in relation to academic learning of certain limited types of knowledge to be regurgitated in examinations at primary and secondary schools—a far cry from the measurement of adult—or even child—capability to carry higher and lower levels of work.

The object of the study we are reporting in this book was to develop a method for the effective evaluation of the potential capability of individuals—both children and adults—to carry given levels of work. We believe that we have succeeded in establishing an objective measure that ordinary, competent adults can be taught to understand and to use with high reliability. It has been validated against the judged potential capability in work of a group of adults of all ages and of a wide range of capability levels, at the above .90 correlation that you would expect of any objective measures in the natural sciences. It is this study and its results that we shall describe.

It should be appreciated from the start that one major consequence of our study is that it will eliminate intelligence tests and will render unnecessary clinical assessments of mental capability. Since intelligence tests have never been satisfactorily validated for predicting capability in work, and since clinical judgments depend upon the clinical experience and ability of the person making the judgment, their elimination is no great loss. But there is another consequence that follows; namely, that if and when the concepts and procedures to be described become widely understood in society, then everyone will know everyone's level of potential capability as an ordinary everyday matter: parents of each other and of their children; teachers of pupils; managers of subordinates, and vice versa; the public of their politicians; and so on and on. It is our firm belief that society would be no worse off. These judgments are currently made *velle nelle:* it is far better that they should be made accurately.

Work, Capability, and Democratic Free Enterprise

The development of an objective measure of the level of work capability in individuals has become an urgent and critical task in the modern world for the following reason. One of the main features of economically developed nations is that they are full-scale employment societies; that is to say, the vast majority of their people who work for a living do so by getting employment for a wage or salary in a managerial hierarchical organization. Except for Great Britain, which developed into a full-scale employment society in the first half of the twentieth century, the other so-called fully developed nations reached full-scale employment society status largely in the second half of the twentieth century. Thus, for example, the United States reached the 93% mark only a few years ago; that is to say, reached the point where 93% of the working population—125 million people in all—were employed in positions in managerial hierarchical organizations, and only 7% were self-employed.

This fact of the coming into existence of the employment society makes urgently necessary an objective method of measuring each person's potential level of capability in work. For the opportunity to get work within employment systems (in contrast to being self-employed), at a level consistent with one's potential capability, rests upon the judgments of that potential by someone else—a manager, or a human resources "expert," or an outside psychological "expert"—and the fact is that there exists no objectively based expertise.

For fully developed democratic free enterprise societies to continue to thrive, they must provide reasonable opportunities for all of their citizens to gain employment at levels that allow them to use their potential capability to the fullest, so that society gains from the full contribution of its peoples' talent and creativity, and each of us can get the enormous satisfaction that comes with the full exercise of our potential in our work. There are equally great consequences for education of having a greater understanding of the true potential capability of our children.

A Fundamental Condition

Any satisfactory measure of potential capability in work requires two things: first, a measure of level of work; and, second, a method of measuring an individual's potential ability to work at a given level of work. In other words, the measure must be such that a person whose potential capability measures x will be found to have the potential to carry a role whose level of work is x, so long as the person values doing that work, has had the opportunity to acquire the necessary skilled knowledge to do so, and is not temperamentally handicapped.

This condition has not been met by any of the so-called measures of intelligence or capability. Thus IQ, used in schools and in selection, appointment, promotion, and career development, does not serve this purpose adequately. And its use in studies purporting to compare the native abilities of racial groups has been unfortunate. One of the problems has been that no validating measure of level of work had been available, until the discovery by one of us that the time-span of discretion of a role gives an objective measurement of its level of work.[1] This measuring instrument has laid the foundation and the conceptual direction for the research into potential capability that we shall describe.

In order to escape from the conceptual shortcomings of the field, we shall turn to the rigorous definition of task, work, and musing; roles and level of work in a role (time-span measurement); organizational stratification; potential capability; applied capability; and maturation of potential capability. We shall then turn in chapter 2 to the issue of mental processing and types of mental processing, and of complexity of work and complexity of mental processes.[2]

A Problem For Our Readers

It has been our experience that our approach creates a substantial problem for the two main categories of our potential readers. On the one hand, there are those with a bent towards cognitive psychology, mainly academic psychologists, who might be interested in those of our findings concerned with cognitive or mental processing, but who are likely to have trouble with findings about work, level of work, and organization, because all that seems so "managerial," or so "applied." On the other hand, there are those who are interested in "the doing of work" and its organization; they can cope with the concepts of task, work, manager, and organization, for they seem real, but they might have trouble with the academic psychological piece or "all this mental processing stuff."

Very few readers are likely to be at home with both sides of our theme—on the one hand, the psychological capability to carry out real

1. Jaques (1956) *Measurement of Responsibility.*
2. For a more systematic elaboration of these concepts, see Jaques (1989) *Requisite Organization,* Jaques (1990) *Creativity and Work,* and Jaques and Clement (1991) *Executive Leadership.*

adult (or childhood) work, and on the other hand, the nature of work itself and the measurement of its level of complexity. This dichotomy is unfortunate, for unless these two aspects are successfully brought together and connected, there is no hope of validating any procedure for evaluating individual capability for real work. It is precisely the failure to be able to bring these two sets of phenomena together that has been the source of such great waste of effort, both in academic psychology and in practical human resources work, for the past seventy-five years. We will attempt to show how resolving this dichotomy opens up new theoretical vistas in our understanding of mental processes, and basic new procedures for the world of management and work. We ask, therefore, for the indulgence of readers who find themselves called upon to cross unfamiliar boundaries in addressing our research.

Three Basic Categories of Human Working Capability

There exists substantial confusion on the subject of individual working capability, because of the common failure to separate out the three main categories of human capability; namely, Current Potential Capability (CPC); Current Applied Capability (CAC); and Future Potential Capability (FPC). In order to avoid this confusion from the start, we shall define these concepts, and will use the terminology consistently. These definitions will be elaborated more fully in chapter 2.

Current Potential Capability (CPC): A person's Current Potential Capability (CPC) is the maximum level of work that that person could carry at any given point in time, not in any work but rather in work that he or she valued doing and had been able to gain the necessary experience and skilled knowledge to perform. It is one of our hypotheses that this potential has at any given age a maximum level determined by the person's maximum complexity of mental processing. Our research focuses upon this aspect.

Current Applied Capability (CAC): Current Applied Capability (CAC) is the level of capability a person is actually applying at a given moment in some specific work. We shall argue that it is a function not only of that person's potential capability, but also of both the intensity of his or her commitment to doing that work, and the extent of his or her experience and skilled knowledge with respect to it. Applied capability can never be greater than potential capability, and will usually be less because of the less than full commitment or of less than the complete experience and skilled knowledge necessary—just as the kinetic energy of a system is less than its potential energy through the wastage effects of friction. It is to be emphasized that a person's current potential capability (CPC) sets that person's current level of work ceiling for any and every type of work, whereas current actual capability always relates to the level of work being exercised in a specific task or role that is currently being carried out.

Future Potential Capability (FPC): Future Potential Capability (FPC) is the predicted level of potential capability that a person will possess at some specific time in the future. We shall present evidence in chapter 7 that potential capability grows throughout life from early childhood to old age along regular and predictable maturational pathways, and that, therefore, the Future Potential Capability of a person (FPC) at given ages can be reliably predicted once that person's Potential Capability at some specific age has been ascertained.

Task, Work, and Musing

Human behavior can be divided into two different and all-encompassing types of activity; namely, *work* or *goal-directed* behavior and *musing* (or reverie or dreaming) that has no *articulated* goal to bound and to direct it.

In order to understand work, it is necessary first to understand what a task is. For work is goal-directed behavior in the sense that the behavior is always directed towards the achievement of some specified output by a targeted completion time; that is to say, directed towards carrying out a task. The task may be preparing a meal or a market analysis; assembling a product or selling it; designing a house or a toy; writing a memorandum or a letter; repairing a car or delivering a packet; teaching a class or developing a training program.

In each case, it must be noted that the task is specified not only in terms of producing one or more of a particular thing, but of a particular thing within a given standard of quality, by a given time, and within given limits of expense and method (i.e., resources). Although quality standards and expense and method limits are not always precisely stated, or even stated at all, they are always implicitly assumed. For without such assumptions, a task is unlimited and simply flaps in the wind.

Equally, a targeted completion time must also always be stated or implicitly assumed in order for a task to exist. For once again if no targeted completion time is assumed, it is impossible to plan and organize to do the necessary work.

We shall thus define a **task** *as a* quantity *(Q) of things within given* quality *limits (Q) to be produced by a* targeted completion time *(T) within specified* resource limits *(R)—in short, as a what-by-when to be achieved within resources; or in even shorter-hand as a QQT/R.* This definition is not innocuous. It underlies the whole of our research. It will become apparent that without this concept, there is no possible solution to the problem of validating an objective measure of the level of work capability of individual human beings.

Now what about the meaning of *work* as compared with *task*. In order to be clear, it is useful to note the following confusion in everyday speech. "That was tough work doing the work they gave me to do at work today"; or, "That was a tough job doing the job they gave me to do in my job today." There are three very different ideas here, masquerading under the same two words. The second idea will be recognizable as the concept of task defined above. As for the other two, we shall use the terms work and work role, giving the following usage: "That was tough *work* carrying out the *tasks* I have been assigned in my *work role.*"

Work, then, is what a person has to do in order to carry out a task. It requires first of all that you understand the goal and the available methods. Given that understanding you have either to be given a pathway to follow, or to plan a pathway that you think will enable you to get to the goal. Then you have to proceed along that pathway, overcoming the unanticipated obstacles that are inevitably encountered on the way, and even modifying or changing pathways in the light of circumstances, in order to achieve your end.

If one considers the above process, it becomes apparent that we are describing a process of exercising continual judgment and discretion in manipulating information and making the decisions that have to be made in order to cope with the obstacles that arise. To put the matter another way, we are dealing with a problem-solving process; that is to say, processing information and solving the problems in constructing a pathway and in overcoming obstacles on the way to reaching a goal.

*Our definition of **work** then, is the exercise of judgment and discretion in making the decisions necessary to solve and overcome the problems that arise in the course of carrying out tasks.*

A major point about problem solving, exercise of judgment, and decision making, is that we are dealing with a process that is not accessible to conscious knowledge and reasoning. Conscious knowledge can be and is used for setting the framework and boundaries within which the process runs and problems are tackled, and for providing information to be taken into account. But what happens at actual choice points and how various possibilities and priorities are determined, remains ineffable. In other words, if you know and can articulate the final reasons for making a decision, you have not made a decision. You have merely calculated an inevitable outcome, much as a computer would do.[3]

One of the consequences of this analysis of work is the conclusion that all work is creative. No two decisions can ever be the same, nor can any decision ever be repeated. Every decision is fresh and new, and you never know what you have decided, until you have actually articulated the decision you have made and have begun irreversibly to put resources into it.

By the same token, there is no such thing as routine work; that is to say, there is no such thing as psychological work that is purely automatic. Even work that with a bit more simplification could be automated or robotized is itself not automatic. If a live individual is doing the work, he or she will still be using judgment that no robot could possibly use. But it may certainly sometimes happen that it becomes possible to reduce the level of the work to the point where all judgment has been removed. At that point it could and should be done by a computer or a robot. For computers and robots do not need to think, cannot think, and never will think: the work they do is mechanical work, and not mental work.

It will be useful to keep in mind the difference between mental work and mechanical work. The work that robots and computers do is mechanical work; that is to say, the force (F) of accelerating a physical mass over a given distance, or $W = FS$. They follow rules made by human beings

---

3. This argument is elaborated in Jaques (1989) *Requisite Organization*, on page pairs 33 to 37.

called programmers, and most certainly do *not* make decisions, at least not in the way human decisions are made. By contrast, the human or psychological work we are describing has to do with the non-verbalizable mental processes and sources of judgment, which cannot be encompassed in the terms of W=FS. We shall show that human work (W) is a function of the force (F) required in mental processing over a given time (T), or W=FT. One way to see the gross differences is to recognize that it is always possible to calculate what a computer will do under given circumstances, whereas human decisions can only be known after they are made. In other words, they are knowable retrospectively. You cannot know what decision you have made until after you have irreversibly made it. Human choices are made by feel or intuition: computers have no intuition or gut feel. The gravamen of these distinctions will become clear as our argument unfolds.

Finally, we can sharpen our description of mental goal-directed work by contrast with *musing* (reverie, dreaming), which has to do with withdrawal from seeking any specific, explicit, articulated goals.[4] Musing is the term we shall use to refer to what happens in our mental processing when we are asleep—or to a large extent when we are dreaming or lost in reverie. We detach ourselves from the reality of conscious, organized perception, and from the reality testing of working towards the achievement of specific goals. Instead of our mental processing being organized in relation to the demands of specific, articulated problem solving and action, they float free. Associations and connections are made that may defy the rules of linguistic structure and of the ordinary commonsense experience and logic of waking life.

Under the conditions of musing, freed from the constraint of the external perceptual field, established mental patternings are unraveled and to varying extents regrouped, so that new connections and ideas can refresh the mental field. It is such new juxtapositions that can lead to our waking up with solutions to problems that seemed insoluble the night before, and to the illogical and unlikely connections that occur in dreams but which seem so reasonable during the dreaming.

---

4. The distinction between goal-directed behavior—or work—and musing is not to be confused with the distinction between work and play. Play is in fact the same as work in that all play is goal-directed behavior; play is work with a particular kind of objective— usually pleasure.

Thus we alternate between the organized, bounded, and controlled mental processing of our waking and working hours with their goal-directed organization, and the logically liberated mental processing of our sleeping, musing world with its temporary removal of the reality-based constraints of conscious perception and of working toward explicit goals.

But working and musing are both essential for human sanity. Working provides for reality testing and mental control applied to what we know. Musing, on the other hand, provides for the shaking apart of the known, and the opportunity to wake up with spontaneously generated new ideas. Thus, although we shall be focusing upon the waking hours activity, we hope it will be clear that we are aware of the great importance of what goes on mentally when organized, goal-directed activity has temporarily been relinquished in sleep, dreams, and reverie. Indeed, it is in these latter activities that it is likely that the early signs of a person's future potential capability manifest themselves—but that is a subject for future study and research.

Work Roles and the Level of Work of a Role

A role is a position in a social network. It is related in specified ways to other roles in the network: for example, husband and wife, manager and subordinate, teacher and pupil, priest and parishioner, waiter and diner. Role relationships set the external framework of mutual accountabilities and authorities that govern the behavior between the incumbents of the roles. For orderly behavior to occur between people, each one must be able to rely upon the other(s) to behave within the understood role expectations. All such behavior is inevitably goal-directed; that is to say, the participants are at work.

The role relationships that will interest us in this study are the manager-subordinate role relationships that are the building blocks of the ubiquitous managerial hierarchy. The reason for this choice is simple and weighty: it is possible to observe and to study directly the tasks assigned by a manager to a subordinate and therefore to look also at the nature of the work that has to be done. For the essence of the manager-subordinate relationship is the clear specification of the tasks to be carried out, and therefore of the nature of the work to be done. This specification occurs through the authority, and the accountability, of the manager to determine the assignment of tasks to the subordinate and the accountability of the manager for the subordinate's carrying out of the tasks by doing the necessary work.

As mentioned above, Jaques discovered in the early 1950s[5] a truly objective measure of what he termed the *level of work* in roles subordinate to managers in managerial hierarchical organizations. He called his measure the *time-span of discretion* of the work in the role.

The concept of level of work is one focal point in our study. It has been defined in *Requisite Organization* (page pair 16) as the felt weight of responsibility in the role—its complexity. It is what is commonly described as "the size of a position," "how 'big' one role is as compared with another," "how big a job a person has," "how heavy the responsibility is in a job." Job evaluation schemes are *supposed* to measure this objectively, but in fact they utterly fail to do so.

The reason it is crucial to have a measure of level of work is that the capability we are considering is the capability to do work. The greater your level of capability, the greater is the level of work you can carry. To validate any measure of level of capability to work, therefore, requires that we have a measure of level of work against which to validate it. Our possession of such a measure means that we have been able to carry out a study of level of capability validated in terms of objectively measurable levels of work. Moreover, as will be seen, it has made it possible to express the measure of capability in units directly relatable to level of work units—something no other available "measure" can do. Thus, for example, an IQ of 92 or 126 or 164 does not relate to any particular level of work. To put it another way, the members of Mensa (a society made up of people with IQs above 160) are not noteworthy for occupying positions that carry a society's highest levels of work, nor are those who successfully occupy the highest levels of work necessarily possessed of equally high IQs.

The measure of the time-span of roles in managerial hierarchies is simple. In essence, it calls for a discussion with the immediate manager of a particular role to discover which of the actual tasks being assigned into that role have the *longest targeted completion times*. Thus, for example, if the longest tasks in a role have a 6-month target completion time, the

---

5. Jaques (1956) *Measurement of Responsibility*, (1961) *Equitable Payment*, and (1964) *Time-Span Handbook*.

time-span of the role is 6 months, and that is its level of work. If the longest task in another role has a 12-month targeted completion time, that is its time-span, and it has a level of work twice the size of the first role. Therefore, time-span is the measure of complexity in each of the roles. It is not necessary in this report to go further in describing the time-span measuring instrument. It is described in the above referenced books. It has also been checked for reliability and validity in a number of independent, controlled research studies, the most important of which were carried out by Dr. Roy Richardson and Dr. David Boals,[6] showing correlation coefficients of .86 to .95 between time-span and experienced weight of responsibility.

Organizational Discontinuity and Stratification

It was through the development of time-span measurement, together with the construction of a coherent conceptualization of the meaning of manager-subordinate relationships, that there was uncovered (in the late 1950s) a universal underlying pattern of stratification in managerial hierarchies.[7] Clear-cut boundaries were found that demarcated the true managerial layers (strata). These boundaries were found at the following time-spans: 1 day, 3 months, 1 year, 2 years, 5 years, 10 years, and 20 years (and probably at 50 years). They were called Stratum I, Stratum II, etc. as illustrated in figure 1.1. This terminology is used throughout the book.

The findings which led to the identification of this universal structure of organizational layering—a natural structure—were as follows. If, for example, you ask people who are working comfortably in roles that measure between 3- and 12-months time-span, who is their *real* manager, they will pick whoever is in the first role above the 1-year time-span. They will make this choice even where there is someone in a role less than 12-months time-span shown as the person's "manager" on the organization chart: any such "in-between" person will be referred to as being a "strawboss" or the "administrator" but not the "real" manager. And there will be the experience of too many layers, with all of its adverse symptoms.

---

6. Richardson (1974) *Fair Pay and Work*, and Boals (1992) "The 'Information Age' as an Un-Informing Social Ideology."

7. Jaques (1965) "Preliminary Sketch of a General Structure of Executive Strata."

This same description of too many layers has been found to apply consistently to all so-called manager-subordinate relationships where the managerial and subordinate roles fall between the boundaries shown; for example, a manager at 4-years time-span with a subordinate at 3-years; or at 8-years and 6-years respectively.

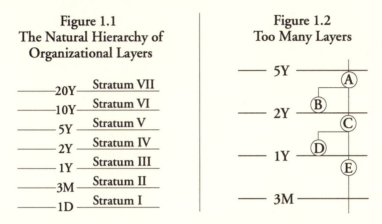

Figure 1.1	**Figure 1.2**
The Natural Hierarchy of	**Too Many Layers**
Organizational Layers	

The import of these boundaries and layers was that it was found to be impossible for anyone in a role with a given time-span to be an effective manager of anyone else in a role with a time-span between the same boundaries; for example, A, who is in a 4-year time-span role, could effectively manage C, in a 21-month time-span role, but not B, in a 3-year time-span role; and C in a 21-month time-span role could effectively manage E in a 9-month time-span role, but not D in a 15-month time-span role. The boundaries appeared to define "states" of managerial work just as the 0° C and 100° C boundaries define states of H_2O (crystal, liquid, and vapor) at sea level.

This finding was at first very puzzling. But evidence accumulated that it occurred in all managerial hierarchies regardless of gross differences in political, economic, or social systems, or of culture generally. The question then was how could this extraordinary set of discontinuities be explained. What was the cause? There appeared to be only one possible answer: it must have something to do with the nature of human nature. For the nature of the human beings involved in the manager-subordinate interaction was the only common factor in all the myriad situations in which the organizational discontinuity was observed. The assumption of the possible relationship between managerial strata and categories of complexity of mental processing was formulated in the early 1960s and described by Jaques in the following terms in 1965:

> The notion that there might be changes in the nature of capacity which accompany increases in the quantity or level of capacity came from the observation of executive hierarchies, in particular, the emergence of new managerial strata at given levels of work as measured in time-span.
>
> Consideration of this phenomenon suggests the hypothesis that these executive strata might correspond to differences in the levels of abstraction which have to be employed in order to make it possible for managerial leadership and authority to be exercised.
>
> If this hypothesis is valid, it would mean that we could expect to find that a manager well established in his or her role would be working at an identifiably different level of abstraction from a subordinate well established in a role one stratum below the manager's. Or looked at in terms of progression, a person would be perceived as becoming ready for promotion to the next higher stratum as he or she began to be able to apply a higher level of abstraction in work.[8]

So the hunt began in 1961 for possible discontinuities in mental functioning that would coincide with managerial stratification. Many hypotheses have been discarded on the way. The aim was to find objectively definable criteria that could be taught, and that would get away from "methods of measurement" that had not been and could not be validated, as well as from clinical procedures that inevitably had to rely upon the clinical skills of each particular evaluator. That aim may now have been achieved. As will be seen, potential capability is quantified in terms of a hierarchy of states of mental processing that turn out to correspond to the hierarchy of managerial strata. Organizational and mental discontinuities turn out to be congruent with each other.

A number of people have made significant contributions to these developments. John Isaac, Roland Gibson, and Brian O'Connor carried

---

8. Jaques (1964) *Time-Span Handbook.*

out experimental studies of problem solving and conceptual analyses of n-valued logic that established the likely existence of discontinuity (discrete levels of abstraction) in problem-solving activity and in the structure of truth-table logic. Gillian Stamp used Isaac's elaboration of the Bruner symbol card sort procedure, and added her own set of phrase cards, to construct a clinical procedure for evaluating current and future potential capability, and has systematically tested her evaluations in substantial follow-up studies.[9] Ian Macdonald developed a parallel set of studies in the mental handicapped field, and demonstrated independently the existence of a series of discontinuous layers of mental processing that corresponded—but at a lower level of complexity of information—with the processes found in managerial systems. It was also Macdonald who suggested that mental processing might be reliably observed in everyday engrossed argument, as, for example, in television debates and discussions. Articles by each will be found in a collection entitled *Levels of Abstraction in Logic and Human Action* edited by Jaques, Gibson, and Isaac.[10]

Against this background, a major step forward was taken by Flynn Bucy in a doctoral research study carried out under the supervision of Dr. J. Harvey at George Washington University. In this study[11] Bucy was able to demonstrate not only that Kohlberg's studies of moral value used in problem solving referred really to categories of cognitive process, but also that these categories corresponded to Jaques' preliminary formulation of his four "cognitive" categories (see *Requisite Organization*). In the course of this study Bucy refined Jaques' formulations, and his work led directly to further refinement of the four types of mental processing used in our research.

---

9. Bruner, Jerome (1966) *Toward a Theory of Instruction.*

10. Jaques, Gibson, and Isaac (1978) *Levels of Abstraction in Logic and Human Behavior.* In addition see Gillian Stamp (1988) "Longitudinal Research into Methods of Assessing Managerial Potential."

11. Bucy (1988) "A Typology of Reasoning Based on Elliott Jaques' Quintave Model of Cognitive Functioning Applied to Moral Problem Solving."

2

Mental Processing
and Complexity

We have had great difficulty over these past few years in deciding upon terminology with which to describe the mental activity or activities concerned with work and with the potential capability for given levels of work. There is certainly no paucity of available terms. The problem lies deeper than that. It is how to understand and describe the processes we are trying to get our hands on. Are we dealing with thinking, feeling, cognition, knowledge, skill, ability, competence, understanding, intelligence, mind, conscious, subconscious, preconscious, unconscious, personality makeup, style, or what? We have switched terminology on many occasions as we felt that somehow we were getting nearer to the heart of the problem.

The following definitions represent where we are at the present time in our thinking. We have decided to switch from the language of cognition and cognitive processes to the language of mental processing. This switch is more than a matter simply of words, or, as it is often put, "of mere semantics." It is a change in concept: from cognitive processes which imply that there are other kinds of related processes involved in mental activity, to the assumption that mental activity is one whole process that cannot be divided into its cognitive aspect plus other aspects. And it does not take an extensive review of the literature on cognition and cognitive "science" to discover that there exists no commonly accepted and used boundary definition of the concept of cognition itself. The only thing that is sure is that it has lost its original pairing with "conation," a term that has almost disappeared from the literature.

A systematic answer to these questions did not emerge until we realized the necessity to differentiate an individual's current potential capability from his or her current applied capability. Current potential relies solely upon the complexity of the on-going problem-solving mental process, and is not affected by knowledge, skill, experience, values, or so-called emotional or temperamental make-up and processes, or of volition or will (what used to be referred to as conation or the conative processes, as contrasted with cognition or the cognitive processes). We therefore developed the following systematic definitions, and shall use them explicitly and rigorously throughout the book.

Potential Capability and Applied Capability

Let us elaborate our definition of capability: the capability we are interested in is **work** or **problem-solving capability**; that is to say, the capability to use discretion and judgment in making the decisions that will enable a person to solve problems in working towards a goal (carrying out a task).[1]

There are three major elements in work capability: first, the level of complexity of mental processing (CMP); second, the extent to which a person values (is interested in) or is committed to the particular work (V); and third, the extent to which a person possesses the necessary skilled knowledge for the particular work (K/S). It will be noted that two elements, values (V) and skilled knowledge (K/S), are specific to particular types of work and roles, and will vary for any given person depending on the role. None of us is omnicompetent, nor equally interested in every kind of work. Only mental complexity (CMP) is generic; we shall argue that it exists as part of a person's makeup regardless of the type of work or of the content of any given role.[2] Value and skilled knowledge operate by influencing how much of a person's potential mental processing can be mustered for particular tasks.

---

1. Jaques, 1956, 1965, 1976, 1989.

2. It is likely that it is this component that the English psychologist Spearman (1922) was seeking to measure in what he referred to as "g" or the general factor in intelligence.

It was our hypothesis that the complexity of mental process (CMP) of any person is an indicator of that person's **current potential capability (CPC)**; that is to say, the maximum capability a person could exercise, given a role the person was really interested in (valued), and for which he or she had had the opportunity to gain the necessary skilled knowledge. Complexity of mental process is the component of capability that we have sought to quantify in our study, because we hypothesize that it is completely congruent with a person's current potential capability. It is the component that causes a person to feel that the level of work in his or her position is right or wrong in the sense of providing the opportunity to work at full stretch. When the complexity of a role matches our current potential capability (CPC) as set by the level of our current maximum complexity of mental processing (CMP), we feel that the role is comfortably big enough. When the complexity of the role is lower than our current maximum potential (CMP), we feel underemployed. When our current maximum potential capability is lower than the task complexity, we feel overstretched.

By the same token, it will be apparent that in order to evaluate the level at which a person could function in some particular role—say, as an accountant or as a production manager—it would be necessary to know not only the level of that person's potential capability, but also how much he or she valued doing that work, and whether he or she had the necessary skilled knowledge for it. Even if the person's current potential capability was sufficient to handle the level of complexity of the work in a given role, he or she might not value the work very highly or might not have sufficient skilled knowledge, in which case full *application* of potential capability would not be possible. Equally, even if a person were enthusiastic about doing accountancy or being a production manager, if s/he did not have the necessary level of complexity of mental process (potential capability) for the task complexity, it would not be possible to succeed in that role.

We shall term the capability to handle the level of work in a particular role—accountant for this branch office, or production manager of that assembly department—a person's **applied capability.** Applied capability comprises potential capability (mental complexity) as a general factor applicable to all work, plus values and skilled knowledge which apply only to any specific role at a specific time. Applied capability will always be lower than potential capability, partly because our values and skilled knowledge are not often just in line with the roles we have the opportunity to occupy at any given time, and partly because the work as assigned by the manager into the role may not provide the opportunity to apply our full potential. It is like potential energy and kinetic energy: kinetic energy (applied energy) will always be less than potential energy because of the waste through friction that occurs in the specific conditions applying in a given situation at a given point in time. Discrepancies between a person's current potential capability, and his or her applied capability in a given role, can equally well be thought of as social friction with attendant social waste. (This theme is pursued further in chapter 8.)

There is a third concept in connection with capability that needs to be included here, but which was not used in our study. It is the concept of *future* potential capability (FPC) against *current* potential capability (CPC). Future potential is the potential capability a person will possess at various times in the future as a result of the maturation of his or her level of complexity of mental processing (potential). Although our study did not deal with the question of future potential, we shall include in our discussion in chapter 7 a description of Jaques' previous work on this subject, in order to illustrate the full significance of our findings. We have had endless trouble with many people with this distinction between current potential capability (CPC) and future potential capability (FPC), because the term potential seems to them to refer to something in the future. In fact, that meaning is not necessarily true. Potential may well refer to present circumstances, as for example, an athlete with the potential to win a certain event, but who cannot realize that potential because of current illness. Indeed, in mechanics the term potential energy refers to the amount of energy currently available for use.

Finally, it may be noted that in our discussion of applied capability we have not referred to the differences in personality characteristics that are often thought to be needed in different types of roles. That omission is not accidental. Personality characteristics are relevant to roles in employment *managerial hierarchies* only insofar as they present themselves in pathological form to a debilitating degree, as for example, abrasiveness or social withdrawal or unreliability to a degree that precludes effective work and working relationships.[3] *We encountered only one such case in our*

---

3. This theme is elaborated in Jaques and Clement (1991) *Executive Leadership*.

study, and did not include it in our results for it was difficult to establish a clear evaluation of current potential.

Mental Processing, Skilled Knowledge, and Values (Commitment)

To summarize, one of the basic propositions of the study is that a person's current potential capability is determined by the level of complexity of that person's most complex mental processing configuration. However, complexity of mental process (CMP) is not the whole story when it comes to the question of the level at which that person can actually apply his or her potential capability to any *particular* type of work or problem. A person's level of *applied* capability in any particular role in a managerial system will be significantly influenced by the degree to which that person values that kind of work and the relevance of his or her skilled knowledge for handling the work, and the quality of relationship with the immediate manager and the tasks he or she is willing to assign.

There is a fundamental difference between a person's potential capability on the one hand, and values (interest/commitment) and skilled knowledge on the other. The difference is that his or her potential capability is an innate property of the person as a whole, whereas a person's values and skilled knowledge are entities that have their own existence in their own right independently of any particular person, and which a person can acquire or shed. Let us elaborate.

Our assumption is that individuals are neither omnipotent nor omniscient, in short, not omnicompetent. At any given stage in our development, there is an absolute maximum level at which we have the *potential* capability to work. That maximum level and its rate of maturation is innate; it is constitutionally in-built from conception. Its maturation is unmodified by education and the amount of knowledge we may have acquired, or by any particular experiences we may have had. An exception might be that maximum potential might be stunted in infancy by gross negative factors such as gross malnutrition. But such deleterious experiences would result not simply in an ordinary lesser level of potential capability, but would appear rather as a damaged or injured or handicapped higher level. We shall have to wait until chapter 7 to explain the evidence for this hypothesis, from studies of maturation. And we would, of course, assume that it is always possible that methods of modifying our maximum potential capability might conceivably be discovered, even though none appear to exist at present.

Our main point is that potential capability, unlike values and knowledge, cannot somehow exist in its own right as a separate entity. It can never have its own freestanding existence. It is always associated with a specific person—as a property of a person—just as color or length exist only as properties of entities and are not themselves freestanding entities.

By contrast, values (interest/commitment) and knowledge can and do have their own existence independent of people. They are objectively recordable, and can continue to exist in recorded form, whether or not they are ever used. They can be taken up by individuals, used or not used, modified, combined with other knowledge or values, stored for eventual use, and gotten rid of. A person's knowledge or values may often be confused with potential capability, in the sense of someone's being judged to be ignorant or knowledgeable in various matters pertaining to work, or "unmotivated" or "motivated" for various kinds of work. Any such confusion between potential capability on the one hand, and knowledge or values on the other, makes for biased or prejudiced judgments against those who have been disadvantaged with respect to education and upbringing for given cultures.

Thus our proposition is that to be able to know our current level of complexity of mental processing is qualitatively different from knowing about the work we value or the skilled knowledge we have. The former is a statement about the person himself or herself. It describes how big in potential capability that person is. By contrast, knowledge and values tell about some of the resources that a person possesses and has available for use. But possession of such resources does not tell you how big the person is or how well the resources will be used, anymore than a person's possessing a lot of money can by itself tell you how big that person is or how effectively he or she may be able to use that money (or to earn any more).

In short, the following is one of the key sets of hypotheses for our current study:

- Current Applied Capability (CAC) for any particular type of work is a function of level of mental complexity (CMP), degree of interest (Value) in that work, possession of the necessary experience and skilled knowledge specific to that work (K/S), and any dysfunctional personal qualities, if they exist (-T).

$$CAC = f\ CMP \bullet V \bullet K/S \bullet (-T)$$

- Current Potential Capability (CPC), i.e., the highest level of work a person could currently carry, in work that he or she valued and for which he or she had the necessary skilled knowledge and experience, is a function of complexity of mental process (CMP) alone.

$$CPC = f\ CMP$$

- Neither the amount of knowledge and experience a person may have acquired, nor the greatest value that person may place upon particular kinds of work, can give a measure of that person's innate maximum current potential capability.

Some Problems of Measurement

An obstacle that has stood in the way of learning how to measure the maximum level of potential capability of individuals at any given age, has been a general approach in psychology that focuses upon people's ability to solve specific problems by providing correct answers to those problems. Thus, for example, in intelligence testing we find how many numbers a subject can repeat, or what words he or she can correctly define, or what series he or she can discover. The problems and answers are standardized, so that scores can be obtained. And so we get mental age (MA), and IQs, and other types of scores.

There are two reasons why this approach presents problems. The first reason is that to know about problems and how to answer them will inevitably be socially influenced—that is to say, influenced by family and cultural background, by education, by language, and by experience. That is why they have been limited to childhood, adolescence, and young adulthood, where there is still a semblance of communality of experience, knowledge, and social outlook for specific social groups. But even in childhood, adolescence, and young adulthood, there are massive differences in background, so that testing has always suffered from the consequences of socio-cultural differences. And certainly no means have been found so far of coping with the outpouring of diversity of experience in adulthood. The result is that there are no quantitative assessments of any kind for adults that can show the growth in capability of an individual with age, as is the case to a limited extent for the evaluation in growth of mental age in children (even though it may not mean much) up to the age of eighteen. Thus it is that psychological research has limited our thinking to the non-validated and counterproductive idea that something called intelligence matures to eighteen years of age, or thereabouts, and then moderately decreases for the rest of one's life.

The second and equally serious shortcoming of the above approach is that it focuses upon answers rather than upon the process—the work— by which the answer was obtained. For right or wrong answers do not by themselves reveal the complexity of the mental processes used to get to them, and they are dependent upon whether or not a subject is familiar with the problems and has acquired the minimum of experience and skilled knowledge necessary to solve them.

When we move from psychological testing that tries to measure a person's maximum capability in general terms, to the more practical assessment procedures used in managerial organizations for promotions and for talent pool development, the picture becomes even less clear. Here one gets into the batteries of tests and evaluation procedures used in their fullest form in assessment center work, and comprising cognitive tests, aptitude tests, personality and preference inventories, interviews, and practical exercises ranging from the in-basket exercise to outdoor individual and group behavioral and problem-solving exercises. The two most comprehensive descriptions of such work, in the sense that they contain systematic and long-term follow-up studies, are the AT&T procedures described by Bray, and the British Civil Service Selection Boards described by Anstey.[4]

There are a number of important shortcomings of this kind of work, from the point of view of the present study, that call for comment. In order to keep these comments in perspective, it is important to keep in mind the central objective of our study; namely, to discover the roots of the *current potential* capability of individuals; how to observe objectively

---

4. Bray (1983) and Anstey (1977).

and reliably and, if possible, measure the direct manifestation of this potential in the dynamics of working behavioral processes; and how to validate the observations in relation to some independent criterion of current potential.

The first problem is that these assessment procedures use unconnected batteries of tests. Since there has been no coherent theory to link these procedures, there is no way of relating the test results to each other. Profiles are used as a basis for discussion among a number of assessors, with consensus among them as the means of achieving a final result.

The second problem is that the procedures are as good as, and no better than, the particular cadre of assessors. Some permanent assessment boards do undoubtedly become expert. But it is never possible to know just how expert, and over what range. During the Second World War, for example, Canadian Army War Office Selection Boards (WOSBs) became expert at evaluating potential combat officers in the sense of producing internally consistent judgments about them, but they never did become comfortable or consistent in their evaluations of potential officers for support and administrative services arms.

The third problem is that assessment centers are used only at critical points in the career development of individuals, such as, for example, in initial recruitment, or at the stage of possible promotion to some higher echelon such as corporate level.

The fourth problem is that these unconnected procedures take the evaluation accountability out of the hands of the immediate managerial system and put it into the hands of a group of people, internally or externally, who cannot be held accountable but whose judgments are foisted upon the managerial system.

The fifth problem is that the highest correlations between board evaluations and attained rank or position at the same time in the future (10, 20, or 30 years) are at only the $r=0.66$ level[5] and in none of such studies has there been a follow-up of those not selected, in the case of intake selection procedures, or, of those who had left the companies, in the case of internal evaluation procedures. Such groups could contain an unknown number of high potential individuals and would therefore reduce the significance of the results.

---

5. Anstey (1977).

Finally, job knowledge was shown in some studies[6] to correlate at 0.78 with eventual performance on the job. But these results were achieved only with subjects who already had the training necessary for the positions for which they were being selected. Therefore, the only conclusion that could be reached was that those who were selected—on some unknown basis—as worthwhile candidates for promotion, were given the training that enabled them to acquire the knowledge necessary for promotion to particular roles. The results could give no information about potential capability, since, for example, all the subjects might have had substantially higher potential than that needed for the roles they were given.

This brief summary of some on-going work illustrates some of the major problems that we have attempted to overcome. In the first place, we sought to get away from procedures that were dependent upon a person's education or cultural background. Second, we sought to develop procedures based upon systematically defined concepts and a coherent theory, so that there could be both a sound basis of construct validity and a contribution to the understanding of the processes involved in human working capability. In so doing, we sought to get through to the core factor or factors determining a person's innate potential capability at any given time, regardless of training or position of the person, or outlooks of the assessors. The theory we have used is that of requisite organization and behavior developed over many years by Jaques and some few associates.[7]

Third, if procedures for evaluating the potential capability of individuals in working organizations are to be requisite, they must be part of the on-going accountability of the managers-once-removed of employees. This proposition conflicts with the common view that each manager should have a possible successor in tow. But it is not the manager who inherits the successor, it is the manager's manager. Therefore, it is the latter who should be accountable for sustaining a talent pool among subordinates-once-removed.[8] We have sought, therefore, not only to add to the understanding of the nature of human capability, but also to get to the kind of basic understanding that can be formulated in everyday terms for

---

6. Hunter and Hunter (1984).

7. See, for example, Jaques (1976) *A General Theory of Bureaucracy* and (1989) *Requisite Organization*.

8. *ibid.*

everyday use by practicing managers. Such knowledge can be used to enhance on-going managerial accountability rather than to undermine it, as is the case with assessment procedures carried out on special occasions by non-accountable internal teams and experts outside the managerial system.

Finally, we wanted to break away from the low standards of what are considered acceptable findings in relation to reliability and validity. Correlations even as high as r=0.66 simply will not do. Such a correlation explains just over 40% of the variance (the square of the correlation), and leaves nearly 60% of the variance unaccounted for. Moreover, the independent variables used to establish the validity of given procedures are uniformly unsatisfactory: they fall far short of meaningful boundary definition; they place nearly exclusive emphasis upon actual capability, and thereby, favoring those who have had education and occupational advantages and are members of favored gender, racial, ethnic, and social groups.

It was, and is, our view, that if it is possible to get to the roots of the nature of innate potential capability, to do so would mean that correlations above r=0.90 both in reliability and validity would regularly be expected, and that the criteria used for establishing validity would relate demonstrably to the potential to carry objectively measurable levels of work. How far we have succeeded in achieving these aspirations may be judged from the results of our study, which is described and discussed in chapters 4 and 5.

The approach we adopted, and the starting point we had available, differed in many respects from current work in the field. We had certain important building blocks: an objective measure of level of work in role (time-span); a system of fundamental stratification of hierarchical managerial work organizations, with boundaries definable in time-span, which could be used as a common framework for the articulation of judgments of potential capability; boundary-defined concepts of current potential capability, current applied capability, and future potential capability; a panoply of rigorously defined organization concepts, including accountability and authority of managers and managers-once-removed with special reference to evaluating potential, succession, and individual and talent pool development; and finally, a systematic and comprehensive set of constructs resulting from the work of the authors and various colleagues

over the past forty-five years, for identifying the mental processes themselves by means of which problems are tackled and work gets done, leaving
aside any reference to the content of the particular problem or the answer
to the problem that is arrived at. That is to say, we were able to focus upon
the pattern of the on-going mental process itself and not whether the
process was the "right" one or a "good" one, or whether the problem was
solved or the "correct" answer obtained.[9] It is to these mental processes
that we shall now turn our attention.

The Four Types of Mental Processing

In simplest outline, we had found that the pattern of people's mental
processing could be observed in the manner in which they organized their
information, or arguments, in the course of an engrossed discussion or
argument in which they were really concerned to set out their point of view
and to make themselves perfectly clear to whomever might be listening.
This idea was suggested by Bucy's work referred to on page 17, building
upon Jaques' concepts of quintaves of cognitive processing.[10]

A first finding was that there were four and only four patterns or types
of mental processing that people use when explaining their position on a
given matter. These four distinct patterns show in differences in the
pattern of the line of thought that is pursued. Any given person, when
engrossed in a problem, would use one of these types of processing as the
overarching or encompassing method of pursuing a point. It may be noted
that in the first three patterns only one position is addressed; in the fourth,
a number of possible positions are compared. The four patterns can be
summarized as follows:

- **Declarative processing:** a person explains his or her position by
  bringing forward a number of separate reasons for it. The reasons
  are separate in the sense that each is brought forward individually,

---

9. A beautiful expression of this problem is to be found in textbooks of dynamics in
physics, to the effect that if you want to study the impact of gravitational forces upon the
acceleration of a free-falling body, there is no use studying the condition of the body after
it hits the ground.

10. Reported in Jaques (1989) *Requisite Organization*, page pairs 33–44.

on its own, and no connection is made with any of the other reasons; for example, "Here's one reason for my idea, here's another, I could give you others as well." This method of processing has a disjunctive, declarative quality.

- **Cumulative processing:** a person explains his or her position by bringing together a number of different ideas, none of which is sufficient to make the case, but taken together, they do; for example, a detective might argue, "If you take this first point (clue), and put it together with these three other items we have observed, then it becomes clear that such-and-such has occurred." This method of processing has a pulled-together, conjunctive quality.

- **Serial processing:** a person explains his or her position by constructing a line of thought made up of a sequence of reasons, each one of which leads on to the next, thus creating a chain of linked reasons; for example, "I would do A because it would lead to B, and B will lead on to C, and C would lead on to where we want to get." This method of processing has a conditional quality in the sense that each reason in the series sets the conditions that lead to the next reason, and so on to the conclusion.

- **Parallel processing:** a person explains his or her position by examining a number of other possible positions as well, each arrived at by means of serial processing (see above). The several lines of thought are held in parallel and can be linked to each other. To take an example, it becomes possible to take useful points from less favored positions to bolster a favored one. "If I start with a possible position that would lead to A and A to B, that would end in outcome 1, which I do not support. Or I could start with another position, that would lead on to C and then to D and get to outcome 2, which I also do not support. I like a third position because it could lead to E and then to F, and that could lead to the outcome 3 that I do favor, but only if you took action B from the first series, and inserted it between steps E and F on the way to outcome 3. This method of processing has a double conditional quality, in the sense that the various scenarios are not only linked with each other, but they can condition each other as well.

Jaques & Cason

Orders of Complexity of the Information Processed

These four types of mental processing have been found to recur at higher and higher orders of complexity of the information itself that is being processed, giving a recursive hierarchy of categories of mental complexity. There are two orders of complexity which could be observed to apply to the levels of work with which we were dealing in the adult employment world, from shop floor to the top executives of large corporations. Then there is a less complex order which could be observed in children from first phases of speech to late adolescence.[11] And then it seemed necessary to assume a still higher order of information complexity at the very top, in the world often referred to as true genius.

A. *First Order Information Complexity—Concrete Verbal (Pointing)*

This is the world of the child from the time it can speak to late adolescence. It is a world in which ideas and their expression in language are concrete in the sense that they are conducted in relation to specific objects that can be pointed to, (or could be pointed to, if they happened to be at some other place at the time). Those who never mature throughout adulthood beyond the ability to handle the concrete order of information complexity are labeled mentally handicapped.[12]

B. *Second Order Information Complexity—Symbolic Verbal Representation*

Concrete things are chunked in verbal information as used in the everyday world of ordinary symbolic discourse. We deal with each other in symbolic, verbal terms without having to point to specific examples of concrete things that we may have in mind. This order of information complexity allows us, for example, to discuss our work, and to issue

---

11. We have recently developed a further hypothesis about the possible existence of an additional order of information complexity used by infants in the pre-verbal first two years. This hypothesis about the four processes showing in gestural behavior is set out in chapter 7, page 93.

12. See the studies by Ian Macdonald (1976) on the stages in development of mental capability in the mentally handicapped. He observed qualitative shifts in methods of mental processing that correspond precisely with the four types of mental processing that recur within each order of information complexity.

instructions to others in a manner that makes it possible to run factories, to design new products, to discuss orders with customers, to record data and get out financial accounts, to maintain information systems, and to carry out all the activities necessary to manage day-to-day work from shop floor (Stratum I) to middle management levels (Stratum IV).

C. *Third Order Information Complexity—Abstract Conceptual*

Here we move into the world of what are commonly called abstract or conceptual ideas. We do not mean abstract in the sense, for example, of the removed-from-real-life-discourse of some academics who may use second order symbolic representation to *talk about* abstract ideas as against actually *using* abstract concepts as a means of overcoming problems. Concepts are used by those with the necessary levels of capability to tackle the complex problems encountered at corporate levels in large corporations or the complexities of large-scale international political problems, as, for example, being able to relate balance of payments, values, international competitive systems, emerging nations, the European Union, the Pacific basin, Japan and the new Far East competition, FOREX (foreign exchange), political economic circumstances in specific countries, treasury policies, raw material resources, and social policies.

D. *Fourth Order Information Complexity—Universals*

Here we move into the world of universal ideas and language used by those usually associated with genius, in handling problems of whole societies, developing lasting philosophies or ideologies, producing artistic masterpieces, or revolutionary developments in scientific theory. The variables are of a complexity well above that required for handling the problems of corporate life. Indeed, one of the outstanding characteristics of those few great corporate leaders who develop super-corporations is that they mature into this fourth order world in their later years, and develop very wide interests, as in the case, for example, of the Konosuke Matsushitas and Armand Hammers of the world.

These propositions about successively higher orders of information complexity are, of course, in line with the notion that different people may live in quite different worlds. Ten people placed in the same situation and faced with a common problem will "see" ten different sets of important features. But those ten different sets of information will not only differ in content, but could also differ markedly in the amount of information constructed from observing and thinking about the situation. Each person will differ in the amount he or she is able to see and to take into account. That is why people capable of working at so-called high levels are commonly described as being able to handle masses of detail rapidly and in an orderly and useful way.

As will become clear, our study has been limited to adults working with second or third order complexity in roles in managerial hierarchies ranging from Stratum I to Stratum VIII. Examples will be given of second order and third order information complexity in appendix A. These examples should make the distinction between the two orders clear.

The Recursive Hierarchy of Categories of Complexity of Mental Process

We have noted that each of the four types of mental processing would recur within each of the orders of information complexity, giving a recursive hierarchy of these processes, much as the seven tones of the standard western musical octaves recur at higher and higher sound frequencies as you proceed from the lower to the higher octaves. In order to simplify our description we shall use the following terms and notations.

A particular mental process within a particular order of information complexity will be called a *category of complexity of mental process*, for example, a symbolic (second order) serial category, or a conceptual (third order) cumulative category. These terms will be shortened for convenience of presentations to the following system of notations. Orders of information complexity will be designated by capital letters as:

A → Concrete Order
B → Symbolic Order
C → Abstract Conceptual Order
D → Universal Order

and the four types of mental process will be designated by numerals as:

1 → Declarative
2 → Cumulative
3 → Serial
4 → Parallel

Thus, the two examples in the paragraph above would be designated as category B3 and category C2, respectively.

In summary, in figure 2.1 we have hypothesized the existence of the following categories of complexity of mental processing:

Figure 2.1
Categories of Complexity of Mental Processing

Category	Order of Information Complexity	Type of Mental Process
D4	Fourth Order Universal	Parallel
D3	"	Serial
D2	"	Cumulative
D1	"	Declarative
C4	Third Order Abstract Conceptual	Parallel
C3	"	Serial
C2	"	Cumulative
C1	"	Declarative
B4	Second Order Symbolic	Parallel
B3	"	Serial
B2	"	Cumulative
B1	"	Declarative
A4	First Order Concrete	Parallel
A3	"	Serial
A2	"	Cumulative
A1	"	Declarative

But before getting too deeply involved in the details of this recursive hierarchy of processes, let us fill in the background of the developments that led to the discovery of the types of mental process and the orders of information complexity. In so doing, we shall also construct the hierarchical system of definable levels of work which we shall use in validating the key proposition of our study; namely, that each category of complexity of mental process coincides with the level of potential capability to carry a particular level of work, and that a person's current highest level of complexity of mental processing can be directly observed, leading thereby to a direct evaluation of that person's current potential capability (CPC) in work.

Let us now try to clarify exactly what kinds of data we are seeking to obtain. In order to do so, it will be necessary for us to define the distinctions we propose to make between a *directly observable entity*, the equally *directly observable states* in which that entity might appear, and the *objective measurement of properties* of that entity. There is a fourth type of data which we shall not address; namely, rateable attributes. This fourth type of data is what psychological research usually makes most use of when it attempts to get quantitative data—as, for example, by the use of questionnaires, opinion scales, and other rating scales.[13]

We can exemplify the issues by reference first to the manner in which we study the material world about us. We start with observable things—or entities. One such entity, for example, is an ice cube. The most common method of *quantifying entities* is by counting; that is to say, simply by counting the number of ice cubes you have.

The *measurement of properties* is illustrated by the acts of measuring the volume, or the weight, or the degrees of temperature, say, of one ice cube. And then we can note that the ice is in fact only one of a number of states in which H_2O appears. It can be found also in liquid (water), and in vaporous state (steam), changing predictably from one state to another at particular boundaries in degrees of temperature. In the temperature range between these boundaries (e.g., from $0°$ to $100°$ C), the H_2O remains in the same state. The reason for bothering our readers with this example is to provide a background against which to demonstrate that mental processes are entities that behave in the same way. The mental processes we shall describe are observable entities, just as observable as any other process—once you know what to look for. These processes undergo changes in state, and as will become apparent, we are hypothesizing that

---

13. This issue of the difference between the direct observation of entities, quantifiable by simple counting, and the objective measurement of properties of entities (quantifiable by direct extensive ratio scale measurement), is developed in detail in Jaques (1982) *The Form of Time*, pages 171 to 195.

these changes in the state of the mental process take place at specific points; namely, when that property of the process called its complexity reaches particular levels.

As we mentioned earlier, the problem of how to measure *degrees* of complexity of mental processes has not yet been solved. We continue to address the problem. Meanwhile, however, we would make two points. The first point, and it underlies our whole study, is that you do not have to measure degrees of temperature to be able to observe the various states of H_2O to know that its temperature probably lies between $0°$ and $100°$ C. No more do you have to be able to measure mental process complexity to observe the various states (categories) in which mental processes may manifest themselves. We will show, especially in chapter 5, not only just what these states are and how to identify them as a fact of ordinary everyday observation, but also that each state has its own particular range of levels of current potential capability even though it is not possible (as yet) to identify the precise level of an individual's CPC within that range. That is to say, if a person is observed to be using a particular type of mental processing, it can be known that his or her CPC falls at a level somewhere within the range for that type of processing, but not precisely where. We will show further that these findings are of substantial theoretical and practical consequence.

It is at this point that our approach to the evaluation of potential working capability in individuals differs from the test and test score approach ordinarily used. Our evaluations will be in terms of straight-forward observation of whether a person is using one type of mental process as against another when engaged in engrossed discussion. We shall not be presenting some kind of test from which a test score can be obtained. We shall be presenting descriptions of behavior which, when understood, will enable the observer to come to see things that have been unobservable up to the present time simply because they had not been identified and formulated. It is like gravitational force: it is not possible to observe its downward pull on everything until you learn to understand its manifestations.

The second point is that we shall be able to make an approximation to a measurement of the particular amounts of complexity that lead to each change in state of the mental processes, by reference to the objectively measurable change points in role complexity (level of work change points measured in terms of the time-span of the role) at which qualitative changes in organizational stratification occur. That is a more difficult subject, however, and is best left for our discussion of our findings.

In short, then, we are proceeding down a new road in the field of psychological studies. We are proposing that the basic data for understanding the complexity of mental processes may come from *observing the form or pattern of the processes themselves as they unfold through time.* This process of observing process may feel strange at first. It takes getting used to. But when you get it, you have it. And as we shall demonstrate from our research, once you learn to observe the patterns of mental processing, the world of human behavior opens up in a dramatically new and different way.

PART II

The Research Project

The Study

We set out to test the following hypotheses:
1. There are four and only four patterns of mental process. These processes are:
    Declarative Processing
    Cumulative Processing
    Serial Processing
    Parallel Processing
2. These processes are readily and reliably observable in everyday life.
3. There is a hierarchy of orders of information complexity. These orders are as follows:
    First Order—Concrete (not tested in the study)
    Second Order—Symbolic (tested in the study)
    Third Order—Abstract conceptual (tested in the study)
    Fourth Order—Universal (not tested in the study)
4. The four patterns of mental process may operate in relation to each order of information complexity, giving a recursive system of categories of mental complexity as shown in figure 3.1.
5. The categories of mental process form a hierarchy of states of mental complexity, and the position in this hierarchy of the highest level of mental process a person can achieve gives a measure of that person's current potential capability (CPC).
6. More specifically, the experimental hypothesis was that the correspondence shown in figure 3.1 would be found to exist between a person's category of complexity of mental processing when fully engrossed in

discussion (dependent variable) and the highest level work role that person was judged to have the potential capability to carry at that time (independent variable):

Figure 3.1
Mental Process and Potential in Terms of Stratum

Dependent Variable	Independent Variable
Judged Category of Complexity of Mental Process	Corresponding Judged Maximum Potential in Stratum of Role
Category B1 Symbolic Declarative	Stratum I
Category B2 Symbolic Cumulative	Stratum II
Category B3 Symbolic Serial	Stratum III
Category B4 Symbolic Parallel	Stratum IV
Category C1 Conceptual Declarative	Stratum V
Category C2 Conceptual Cumulative	Stratum VI
Category C3 Conceptual Serial	Stratum VII

Finding a Criterion of Validity

The problem in finding a criterion of validity was to find a way of obtaining an adequate evaluation of a person's current potential capability against which to validate the possible significance of complexity of mental processing. This problem is far from new. It is one that has plagued the validation of measures of intelligence and of capability ever since the early days of Binet and Simon. The variables used as a criterion for establishing validity of methods of evaluating individual capability have always been questionable, ranging from comparisons between average scores for children of the same age in child development studies, to achieved occupation level in studies of adult capability.

The weakness in using achieved occupation level as a criterion lies in the fact that the concept of occupation level is generally defined in terms of job title, it being assumed that positions with the same titles are necessarily at the same level of work. That assumption is, of course, false.

If positions G and H have the same title, three consequences are possible: G is at a higher level, in a more complex, more difficult, and more responsible role than H, or they are by and large at about the same level, or H is at a higher level than G. But the title certainly does not tell you which. Because of these weaknesses in validation criteria, the validation results can give only approximations, the degree of approximation being inevitably uncertain.

And there is a still more serious difficulty. Even if role title did give a reasonable approximation to achieved occupational level, it would still indicate only the actual level at which a subject was currently working, and could in no way indicate whether or not that level reflected any given individual's current *potential*, and that was what we were interested in. This same criticism would apply also to two- or three-day assessment center procedures. For even there, where observation is possible of individuals in actual problem-solving situations, the same shortcoming applies. There are no common markers or criteria against which to state judgments about current potential capability, other than these same ill-defined position titles, or equally ill-defined grades. It can never be ensured, therefore, that different evaluators are using the same standards of judgment.

It occurred to us that practical project work in which we were engaged in the field of talent pool development might provide an answer to the validation problem. In this work, the current potential capability of employees was being evaluated and periodically reviewed by their manager-once-removed (MoR). These evaluations were discussed with each employee by his or her MoR as part of a mentoring and career counseling process, so that the employee also had the opportunity systematically to think about his or her potential capability, to evaluate it, and periodically to review that evaluation. Moreover, these evaluations were being made systematically against a background of roles with objectively measurable levels of work placed within a common structure of layers (strata).

We thus had circumstances in which we could get judgments about individuals' current potential capability where the evaluations counted in a very serious way. These judgments were founded upon a long-term view of the individuals by people who had experience of them at work; were periodically reviewed; were checked against actual use in transfers from one position to another and in upgrading and promotions; and were formulated in relation to a single system of assessed levels of work of the roles in relation to which they were being evaluated.

We had the possible makings of a solid foundation of evaluation of current potential of individuals in work situations. If under the conditions described in the previous paragraph, you had agreement between an employee, that employee's immediate manager, and the employee's manager-once-removed, that the employee had the current potential to work at a particular level—say Stratum II—that would be about as good an evaluation of that person's current potential as you could get, for it would be grounded upon actual experience of the individual engaged in work of known level, but would not be fixed at this level if the individual's current potential capability (CPC) differed from current applied capability (CAC) because of limitations of opportunity. It would certainly be a marked improvement on the independent variables that had been used for validation purposes in research up till now. We decided to proceed with such a threefold judgment as our criterion for current potential capability, for our previous experience had consistently shown that under the serious conditions described, there was a strong possibility of finding agreement—contrary to common expectation.

The Participating Companies

We therefore sought and obtained the collaboration of two companies, one in the United States (Cason interviews) and the other in Australia (Jaques interviews), in the following systematic and controlled study.[1] The reason for selecting these two companies was that they have both been organized since the early 1980s, in accord with the stratified system of organizational layers as described in the previous chapter. Both are Stratum VII companies; that is to say, the roles of their CEOs actually measure at above 20 years in time-span, and they have seven organizational layers in all, including the company CEO and the shop and office floor.

---

1. The North American company is Gilbert Commonwealth in Reading, PA, and Atlanta, GA. It provides design, construction, and technical services to the power generating industry, and employs about 5,000 people. The Australian company is CRA with mines, smelters, and production throughout Australia, the Pacific basin, Europe, and the United States. It employs about 25,000 people.

In addition, both companies have pursued policies and procedures in which the accountabilities of the immediate managers and of managers-once-removed have been differentiated in a requisite manner. A manager (B) is held accountable for the output of immediate subordinates (Cs) and for appraising their working effectiveness and coaching them so as to increase that effectiveness. Managers-once-removed (As), by contrast, are held accountable for developing successors to immediate subordinate roles, for evaluating the potential capability of their subordinates-once-removed (Cs) for progress to the next higher stratum, and for the mentoring and career development of their subordinates-once-removed.[2]

Judgments of Current Potential

We thus had especially favorable circumstances for our study in these two companies. Our subjects (with some exceptions) had been officially evaluated by their manager-once-removed at least once and, in most cases, on a number of occasions over periods of up to seven years, in terms of judgments about both their current and their future potential capability. For purposes of the study, each subject's own personal evaluation of his or her current potential was also obtained, plus further supportive information in the form of the immediate manager's evaluation of the subject's current and future potential. It is in connection with these judgments of current and future potential that the existence in both companies of a requisite structure of organizational layers was of such over-riding importance. All judgments could be formulated in the same terms, in accord with the following procedure:

With respect to judging an individual's *current potential* capability, one question, and one question only, was asked: namely, "If X were in a role with work that he or she really valued doing and had had the opportunity to gain the necessary knowledge and experience for the work, at what stratum (organizational layer) do you judge X would be capable of working at present?"

The judgment had to be made in terms of the highest stratum (organizational layer) which the individual was deemed to have had the

2. See Jaques (1989) *Requisite Organization,* and Jaques and Clement (1991) *Executive Leadership,* for a detailed account of these requisite managerial leadership practices.

current potential to occupy in some particular function that would be of strong interest. By using the common organizational strata as the reference points, it could be properly assumed that everyone making the judgments was applying the same frame of reference. Everyone engaged in the study had been familiar for four or more years with the organizational structuring that was being used. Thus, for example, although a Stratum III role might mean Stratum III manufacturing unit manager role to some, a Stratum III house account sales representative role to others, a Stratum III senior production engineering project role to still others, and so on, nevertheless, all were able to attach a common meaning to Stratum III. It meant a role with a measurable time-span between one year and two years, in a stratum immediately subordinate to a general manager in a Stratum IV role between 2-year and 5-year time-span. And if the role was a managerial role, the incumbent would have immediate subordinates in roles at Stratum II ranging from 3-months to 1-year time-span.

Moreover, since time-span gives an objective measure of level of the complexity of work, all of the judgments of potential capability were thus being made in relation to a commonly held concept of the level of work—identical in both of the participating companies—that an individual had the potential capability to carry. It is in this fact that judgments of capability were made in terms of a rigorously established concept (and objective measure) of level of work, that our study with respect both to validity and to reliability differs from other comparable studies.

We have thus taken two significant steps forward. The first step was to use judgments about the current *potential* capability of our subjects; that is to say, by the level at which they were judged to have the capability to work currently, in work that they valued, and for which they had had the opportunity to gain the necessary skilled knowledge, rather than in terms of the level at which they were currently being employed—a person's true level of current potential capability being far from necessarily reflected in his or her current employment opportunity. The second step was to get the participation of two companies in which the real level of work was known in each position regardless of title, so that all roles could be objectively compared with each other, regardless even of the countries in which the positions were placed.

By proceeding in this manner, we had information not only about the level at which each subject was actually working, but also about the level at which each was judged to have the potential to work, regardless of whether or not there was a discrepancy between the two levels.

The judgments of potential were most commonly stated in terms of the potential to work at a specific stratum, for example, Stratum III. But in approximately 15% of the cases, the judgments were made in terms of a subject's being perceived as on one of the boundaries; for example, "just on the boundary of Stratum III and Stratum IV" or, "just moving from Stratum III to IV, not fully in IV yet, but not fully in III either." We recorded such judgments as boundary judgments, for example, III/IV. As will be seen, the researchers also found it necessary to make such boundary judgments.

The Population in the Study

Because of the precision of the various categories of data used in the study, and because of the very high correlations that were expected, it was determined that 30 subjects, 5 each from roles in Stratum I to Stratum VI, would be sufficient for significant results. In the end we decided to double this number. The basis of selection was simple. Each Stratum VI manager chose several of his or her subordinates at Stratum V, who in turn selected several of their own subordinates, and so on down to Stratum I. We ended up with 72 subjects in the study—39 from six Stratum V subsidiary units in the Australian company; 33 from two Stratum V subsidiary units in the U.S. company; and two subjects from Stratum VI chosen by a toss of the coin to ensure total anonymity.

Because there would be no possibility of protecting the confidentiality of the two Stratum VII CEOs, their inclusion was not sought. Instead, two CEOs were found who were currently working successfully at Stratum VII in two other unnamed companies, and another two CEOs from two other organizations currently working at Stratum VIII. These data were obtained only for the purpose of filling out the top end of our study; they were not included in our results. We shall, however, include examples of the nature of the mental processing of one of each of these pairs for illustrative purposes only, to show what mental processing looks like at these high levels.

All of the subjects were asked by their managers if they would "volunteer" for the study. We are quite aware of the difficulties in which subordinates are placed if they do not wish to accede to such a request. It was possible, however, to resolve this difficulty readily. Both of the researchers were well known in the companies, and in particular had firmly established reputations for being able to maintain absolute confidentiality. This reputation made it possible to begin each discussion by assuring each subject of a "double" confidentiality. First, the discussions would be confidential in the sense that nothing about the individual would be reported to anyone else. Second, the results of the discussion would not be reported even to the individual, since in the absence at that time of a validation of the procedure, it would be improper to influence him or her with the specific result.

Following this statement about confidentiality, we explained the purpose of the study, and then gave each subject the opportunity to withdraw. They could readily do so without its being known to anyone else, because no one but ourselves would ever know who had actually taken part in the discussion during the interview period. Two subjects took advantage of this opportunity to opt out.

Sixty-two (86%) of the subjects were male Caucasian. There were seven women and three non-Caucasian males. Four of the women were in positions at one stratum below their judged current potential; two had chosen this situation and two were frustrated. Two of the three non-Caucasian males were employed at full potential and one was underemployed. However, because of the small numbers, no general conclusions could be drawn.

The Procedure

Our procedure was to ask each subject to discuss two topics. First, we asked them to pick a topic on any subject at all, but it had to be a subject that they had a burning interest in, something they were really concerned about. Second, we asked them to tell us what they thought about the possibility of legalizing the use of drugs. We picked legalization of drugs as our standard question because of the general concern in both countries about the subject.

As the participants discussed each topic, the interviewer would interject questions of clarification, alternative arguments, or other comments to help keep the subject well engrossed in the discussion. As can be seen by the illustrations in the addendum, a wide range of topics was chosen for the free choice question. Our subjects reported being strongly engrossed through most of the discussion of both topics, and certainly appeared to be so.

At the end of each discussion the interviewers recorded their judgments of the category of mental complexity displayed in the way each subject processed the information he or she presented. Following that they discussed with the subjects their own judgment of their current potential capability. Although they were not asked, a number of subjects commented on the extent to which they considered that their current potential was fully utilized in their role, or whether they felt underutilized or over-progressed.

All the discussions were tape-recorded, and the recorded material subsequently typed.

Mode of Analysis of the Material

Each of us checked our own interview material to identify in detail the evidence for our judgments of category of mental process. Each then read the typed records of the other's interviews and from those records made and recorded an evaluation of which was the highest category of mental processing that each subject was using, and thus the stratum we predicted the subject would be judged to have the current potential to work at. The judgments were made in terms of a specific category (e.g., cat. B3), or on the boundary between categories (e.g., cat. B2/B3).

A third person who had no previous experience in this mode of analysis was taught the categories and how to recognize them in the transcripts. The ease and rapidity with which high reliability was achieved are described with the results in chapter 5.

The researchers' evaluations of the category of mental process of each subject were compared with the evaluations made by the subjects, their managers-once-removed, and their managers, and an analysis of consistency with which the key hypothesis was conducted. It was assumed that the degree of consistency would give a measure of the validity of observed mental process as a method of evaluation of judged current potential capability in individuals.

4

Results of the Study

The objective of the study was to assess the validity of a new method of evaluating the current potential capability of individuals. Before setting out the results of the study, let us note three key definitions and the key hypothesis to be tested.

Current potential capability (CPC) was defined as the maximum level at which a person could work, given that the person valued the work and had had the necessary education and experience to acquire the skilled knowledge to do it.

The *validation variable* (the variable against which the evaluation method was being validated) comprised judgments of current potential capability of the subjects made by each subject and each subject's manager-once-removed and immediate manager (not in all cases) in terms of the highest possible stratum at which the subject was considered to have the current potential to work; these judgments were based upon actual experience of the subject at work and in progression in level of work over periods of two years and longer.

The *evaluation method* under test comprised judgments of the current potential capability of the subject made by the researchers in terms of an evaluation of the category of complexity of mental process used by the subjects when engaged in engrossed discussion during the experimental interview.

The *key hypothesis* under test was that there would be a one-to-one correspondence between each category of complexity of mental process and one specific stratum of judged maximum potential; that is to say, all

subjects judged to be processing at a given category of mental complexity
would be judged to have the potential to work at one specific stratum as
shown in the list of predicted correspondence in figure 4.1.

Figure 4.1
Hypothesis of Correspondence Between
Evaluation Method and Validity Variables

Evaluation Method Under Test	Validation Variable
Judged Category of Complexity of Mental Process Cason/Jaques	**Judged Maximum Potential in Terms of Role MoR/Mgr/Subject**
Category C3: Conceptual Serial	Stratum VII
Category C2: Conceptual Cumulative	Stratum VI
Category C1: Conceptual Declarative	Stratum V
Category B4: Symbolic Parallel	Stratum IV
Category B3: Symbolic Serial	Stratum III
Category B2: Symbolic Cumulative	Stratum II
Category B1: Symbolic Declarative	Stratum I

Background Data

There was a total of 72 subjects in the population studied. The
distribution of the population by age is shown in figure 4.2.

Figure 4.2
Distribution of Population by Age

The distribution of the population by the organizational stratum of the role they occupied is shown in figure 4.3.

Figure 4.3
Distribution by Stratum of Roles Occupied by Subjects

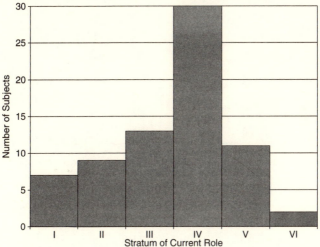

Summary of Data

A summary of the results of the study is presented in figure 4.4. This figure shows the following information for each subject:
- The stratum of each subject's current role.
- The stratum at which each subject's MoR judged that he or she had the current potential capability to work.
- The stratum at which each subject's immediate manager judged that he or she had the current potential capability to work.
- The stratum at which each subject judged he or she had the current potential capability to work.
- Cason's judgment of potential capability based upon the subject's mental processing.
- Jaques' judgment of potential capability based upon the subject's mental processing.
- Comments made by the subject.

Figure 4.4
Summary of Results

Subject	Stratum of Role	Validation Variable			Category of Mental Process		Subjects' Comments
		MoR	Mgr	Self	Cason	Jaques	
1	I	I/II	II	I/II	B2	B2	Frustrated
2	I	II	II	II	B2	B2	Moving Up
3	I	II	-	II	B2	B2	
4	I	II	II	II	B2	B2	Resentful
5	I	II	II	II	B2	B2	Underemployed At Own Choice
6	I	II	-	II	B2	B2	
7	I	I/II	II	II	B2	B1/B2	
8	II	II/III	II/III	II	B3	B2/B3	
9	II	II	II	II	B2	B2	
10	II	II	II/III	III	B3	B3	
11	II	III	II/III	III	B2/B3	B2/B3	
12	II	IV	III/IV	III/IV	B3/B4	B3/B4	Frustrated
13	II	II	II	III	B3	B2	
14	II	III	II	III	B2/B3	B2	
15	II	III	III	III	B3	B3	
16	II	III	III	III	B3	B3	
17	III	IV	III	IV	B3	B4	Frustrated
18	III	III/IV	III/IV	III/IV	B3/B4	B3/B4	
19	III	III	III	III	B3	B3	
20	III	III	-	III	B3	B3	
21	III	III	-	IV	B3	B3	
22	III	IV	IV	IV	B4/C1	C1	
23	III	IV	IV	IV	B4/C1	B4/C1	
24	III	III	III/IV	III/IV	B3/B4	B3/B4	

(continued on following page)

Jaques & Cason

Figure 4.4
Summary of Results *(continued)*

Subject	Stratum of Role	Validation Variable			Category of Mental Process		Subjects' Comments
		MoR	Mgr	Self	Cason	Jaques	
25	III	II/III	-	II/III	B2	B3	
26	III	III	III	III/IV	B3/B4	B3	
27	III	III	III	IV	B3	B4	Looking For Promotion
28	III	IV	-	IV	B4	B4	
29	III	III	III	III	B3	B3	
30	IV	IV	IV	IV	B4	B4	
31	IV	IV	IV	IV	B4	B4	
32	IV	IV/V	-	IV/V	C1	B4/C1	
33	IV	V	V	V	B4/C1	C1	
34	IV	IV	III	IV	B3/B4	B3	
35	IV	IV	IV	IV	B4	B4	
36	IV	IV	IV	IV	B4	B4	
37	IV	IV	IV	IV/V	B4/C1	B4/C1	
38	IV	III	III	III	B3	B3	(MoR)Failing
39	IV	IV/V	IV	IV/V	B4/C1	B4	
40	IV	IV	V	IV	C1	C1	
41	IV	IV	-	IV	B4	B4	
42	IV	IV	IV	IV	B4	B4	
43	IV	V	IV/V	V	B4/C1	C1	Frustrated
44	IV	IV	IV	IV	B4	B4	
45	IV	IV	III	IV	B4	B4	
46	IV	IV	IV	IV	B4	B4	
47	IV	IV	IV	IV	B4	B4	
48	IV	IV/V	IV/V	V	B4/C1	C1	

(continued on following page)

Jaques & Cason

Figure 4.4
Summary of Results *(continued)*

Subject	Stratum of Role	Validation Variable			Category of Mental Process		Subjects' Comments
		MoR	Mgr	Self	Cason	Jaques	
49	IV	IV	IV	IV	B4	B4	
50	IV	IV	-	IV	B4	B4	
51	IV	IV	-	IV	B4	B4	
52	IV	IV	IV	V	C1	C1	
53	IV	IV	IV	IV	B4	B4	
54	IV	IV	IV	IV	B4	B4	
55	IV	IV	IV	IV	B4	B4	
56	IV	IV	IV	IV	B4	B4	
57	IV	IV	-	IV	B4	B4/C1	
58	IV	IV/V	IV/V	V	C1	C1	
59	V	IV/V	V	V	C1	C1	
60	V	V	V	V	C1	C1	
61	V	V	-	V	C1	C1	
62	V	V	V	V	C1	C1	
63	V	IV/V	V	V	C1	B4/C1	
64	V	V	V	V	C1	C1	
65	V	V	IV/V	V	C1	C1	
66	V	IV	IV	IV	B4/C1	C1	
67	V	V	V	V	C1	C1	
68	V	VI	VI	VI	C2	C2	
69	V	V	V	V	C1	C1	
70	V	V	VI	VI	C2	C2	Bursting Out
71	VI	-	VI	VI	C2	C2	
72	VI	-	VI	VI	C2	C2	

Reliability of Judgments of Potential Capability in Terms of Stratum (Validation Variable)

A similar type of criterion of reliability (inter-rater judgments) to that shown in figure 4.5 was used for judgments between each subject and the subject's manager-once-removed (MoR) and manager (where available) of the stratum at which they judged the subject to have the current potential capability to work; namely, judgments of current potential capability (CPC) that placed a subject in the same stratum, e.g., Stratum III, or at the upper or lower boundary of that stratum e.g., Stratum II/III or Stratum III/IV, were considered consistent. Between the MoR and the subject, there was a correlation of .96; between the manager and subject, a correlation of .95; and between the MoR and manager, a correlation of .94. There were 27 boundary judgments out of the total of 204 judgments; a total of 14%.

Figure 4.5
Reliabilities of Inter-Rater Judgments

Judgments between	Number of Cases	Correlation r
KC and EJ (Categories of Mental Process)	72	0.95
MoR and Subject (Subject's Potential Stratum)	70	0.96
Mgr and Subject (Subject's Potential Stratum)	60	0.95
Mgr and MoR (Subject's Potential Stratum)	58	0.94

Reliability of Judgments of Mental Process by a Newly Trained Observer

A third observer, who knew nothing about the concepts being tested, was trained in how to recognize the mental processes under analysis. The aim was to discover whether others could learn the process, how easy it would be, and how reliable the results might be as compared with the judgments of the authors.

The first step was a two-hour discussion to explain the concepts, and to illustrate them from case material. Following this discussion, the third observer was given eight protocols, which she read and judged in terms of category of mental process. Of the eight judgments, six coincided with the researchers' judgments (75%).

This procedure was repeated twice more with similar results. Finally, the observer was given fifteen protocols to judge: thirteen judgments coincided with the judgments of the researchers in category of mental process (87%). Supporting evidence that these concepts can be effectively communicated at least to individuals at B3 level of potential and above comes from the fact that the researchers have taken five managers through the above teaching process with similar reliability of outcome.

Evidence Supporting the Key Hypotheses

The key hypothesis which the study was designed to test is specified on page 51 above and summarized in figure 4.1. A perfect correlation in support of the hypothesis would be one in which, when the independent variable (the ratings of potential made by the MoR, the manager and the subject) gave a CPC for the subject of Stratum I, II, III, IV, V, or VI, then the dependent variable (the evaluations by the authors of category of mental process) would show category B1, B2, B3, B4, C1, and C2, respectively.

The correlations are shown in figure 4.6. The most significant finding is the correlation of .97 in support of the hypothesis for the 60 cases in which we had judgments made by all three, the manager-once-removed (MoR), manager, and subject. This correlation is reinforced by a correlation of .96 when the subjects' own judgments (72 cases) were taken as the independent variable; and a correlation of .94 for the MoR's judgments alone (60 cases).

From these results we conclude that our hypothesis is strongly supported. The category of mental processing employed by our subjects gives a measure of the current potential capability (CPC) of these subjects as judged by highly reliable ratings of that potential capability made by the MoR, manager, and the subject, in terms of the stratum at which the subjects were judged to have the potential capability to work (i.e., given the opportunity to get the necessary skilled knowledge and experience to do so).

Actual Stratum and Judged Potential Capability

There were high correlations of .89 to .91 between the actual stratum occupied by subjects and their judged potential capability. The variances ranged between .80 and .82. Strikingly, however, where there were discrepancies between the actual stratum and the judged potential of individuals, the judgments of potential derived from the judged categories of mental processing coincided with the independently made judgments of potential rather than with the actual role occupied.

Figure 4.6
Correlation Between the Sets of Judgments of Potential Capability[1]

The Sets of Judgments of Potential Capability	Number of Cases	Correlation r
Average (MoR • Mgr • Subject) and Average (KC • EJ)	60	0.97
Subject and Average (KC • EJ)	72	0.96
MoR and Average (KC • EJ)	70	0.94
Mgr and Average (KC • EJ)	60	0.93

Figure 4.7
Correlations Between Stratum of Actual Role and Judged Potential of Subject

Judgments	Number of Cases	Correlation r
Role Stratum and Average of MoR and Subject's Judgment	70	0.91
Role Stratum and MoR's Judgment	70	0.89
Role Stratum and Average of KC • EJ	72	0.89

1. Pearson product-moment correlations carried out using a Lotus spread sheet.

5

Discussion of Results

Our findings suggest there is a strong case for the following conclusions:

1. There are four and only four patterns of mental processing used by individuals when engaged in engrossed discussion, as shown by the fact that these four patterns recur within different orders of complexity of information, giving a stepwise series of categories of complexity of mental process.

2. The discrete steps in categories of complexity of mental processing can be reliably seen by trained observers. Indeed our sense is that with increasing experience and with multiple opportunities to hear any given person engaged in engrossed discussion, practically 100% reliability will be achieved.

3. There are at least two different orders of complexity of information used by adults in engrossed discussion.

4. The four methods of mental processing can be observed in each of the two different orders of information used by the adult subjects; they are recursive and maintain their hierarchy of complexity.

5. The category of complexity of mental processing used by individuals, when engrossed in discussion of subjects of interest to them, gives a valid judgment of the highest organizational stratum at which they have the current potential to work given the necessary opportunity.

6. There is one category of complexity of mental processing that matches the span of level of work for each specific organizational stratum in the managerial hierarchy.

Possible Explanations of Results

It might be agreed that there is an exceptionally strong relationship between our independent and dependent variables in support of our basic hypothesis of a unique relationship between each stratum of judged potential capability and each category of complexity of mental processing. By the same token, the independent judgments of MoRs, managers, and subjects with respect to each subject's current *potential* capability are extremely close.

Our hypothesis, of course, is that our two sets of variables are expressions of the same thing; namely, judgments of individual *potential* capability as conjectured or construed from the work situation, alongside that same potential capability as expressed in mental processing during engrossed discussion. But might not the subjects' actual levels of work or their level of knowledge explain the results? Let us examine these possibilities.

Relation Between Stratum of Subjects' Current Role and Judged Potential

The correlations between the stratum of the role actually occupied by the subjects, and the stratum they were judged to have the potential to occupy, are shown in figure 4.7; although not as high as the correlation between the two separate sets of judgment of potential, they were nevertheless impressively high. They give some evidence of two companies which have procedures for getting full utilization of the potential capability of their employees and which are using these procedures to provide such opportunities. There was a correlation of .91 between the stratum occupied by the subjects and the stratum they were judged by the MoR and the subject to have the potential capability to fill; a similar correlation for the MoRs' judgments alone of .89; and a correlation of .89 with the judgments of potential made by the authors in terms of category of mental process.

But do these high correlations not suggest that the high correlations supporting the key hypothesis merely reflect the actual stratum at which the subjects were working? In other words, was the high correlation between the dependent and independent variables a reflection of actual stratum operating as an overriding intervening variable? The answer to this question is no, for a number of reasons of considerable interest.

In the first place, and most importantly, Cason and Jaques each knew the stratum of the role occupied by each of the subjects they personally interviewed (Cason in the United States company, Jaques in the Australian company). They did not have that information about the subjects of each other's interviews. The high reliability of their ratings demonstrates little or no influence of knowledge of subjects' stratum of current role upon their judgments. In other words, the two researchers came out with substantially the same judgments of the potential of subjects whether or not they knew the stratum of their current role; that is a clinching argument.

Second, the high correlation between the two sets of variables indicates that wherever the MoR, manager, and subject agreed that a subject was underemployed (i.e., in a role at a stratum below judged current potential), then the researchers also found that such underemployment existed.

Third, in the ten cases where the subjects spontaneously expressed opinions concerning the degree of their satisfaction with their current roles, these opinions were in line with what might be expected. Of the nine who were underemployed, six expressed frustration, one had sought underemployment for domestic reasons, one was actively seeking promotion, and one, who had been notified of an impending promotion, expressed strong satisfaction. The tenth was a case of an individual who had been overpromoted, and all the five judgments (MoR, manager, subject, and two researchers) were consistent in rating current potential one stratum below current role; steps had already been taken by the MoR to arrange a transfer to a role more in keeping with judged potential, to the relief of the subject as well as the manager.

And finally, whereas actual stratum might conceivably influence MoRs' and managers' judgments of the potential capability of subordinates, it would be far less likely to influence the judgments, under conditions of absolute confidence, of those subordinates themselves. The shared consistency (inter-rater reliability) of the judgments of the MoRs, managers, and subjects is striking. We can be sure that the subjects were offering true judgments of their *potential* capability: it was not in their interest to do anything else. So, therefore, must the MoR and manager judgments be in line with potential capability rather than actual role. And as for the fact that subjects apparently did not inflate their judgments of their potential capability, that is a phenomenon that both authors are quite used to. Despite common belief to the contrary, given half a chance to state their true judgments of themselves without having to impress others, people are both realistic and accurate in those judgments. Unfortunately, the abysmal social and psychological conditions under which we manage our employment systems do not often provide for such constructive conditions.

Possible Impact of Knowledge

Nor can the amount of knowledge possessed by our subjects have had a significant impact upon our results. In the first place, the complexity of mental processing used in the discussion of legalization of drugs was the same for all subjects as the complexity of mental processing they used in discussing the topic of their own choice, despite substantial differences in knowledge about the topic. Second, it was not the case that those subjects judged to have a higher level of potential, or seen as using more complex mental processing, necessarily had greater knowledge about the drug problem. Knowledge varied with interest in the topic rather than with potential capability. Indeed, three of our subjects at current potential Stratum III (cat. B3), and three at Stratum IV (cat. B4), had extensive knowledge through direct involvement in drug prevention programs as compared with the knowledge available to any of our thirteen subjects at current potential Stratum V (cat. C1) and Stratum VI (cat. C2).

Therefore, our evidence is that each person's own maximum complexity of mental processing can be applied in considering problems of interest so long as he or she has enough knowledge with which to put a case together. Greater amounts of knowledge, however, do not increase the complexity of mental processing.

This conclusion once again emphasizes that we are studying current *potential* capability to work at a given level of work, even though a person may not yet have acquired the necessary amount of knowledge to work in one or another specific role at that level. The proposition is that given the necessary potential capability (mental complexity) a person can acquire the necessary skilled knowledge to work at a given level in a role whose work is of interest (valued). The converse, however, is not true. A person's level of potential capability is determined by maturation only, and that maturation is independent of the person's level of skilled knowledge and valuing of the role. Moreover, potential capability (mental complexity) is not only independent of any particular acquired knowledge and values, but also determines how much of a person's acquired knowledge can be usefully employed, and how that knowledge will be used in work.

A Most Likely Explanation of the Results

In the light of the above analysis, our view is that the strong relationships between, on the one hand, the MoR, manager, and self judgments of *potential* capability of subjects to work at a given stratum, and on the other hand, their judged category of complexity of mental processing, are a true and direct expression of the operation of what we have defined as their *current potential capability.*

Our evidence is, therefore, that this potential capability can be evaluated accurately by individuals themselves, and by close-at-hand managers who know them. What it is that is observed, however, and how these judgments are made, like all judgments, could not be articulated. Phrases were used like: "Is very imaginative"; "Has begun to take a wider interest in things here at work"; "I left him to deputize for me when I was away a few months ago, and although he wasn't perfect, he did keep things together"; "I had him work directly with me (the MoR) half time, on a project, and I was very impressed by his potential"; "She is well-educated, and has shown that she can hold her own very well at work on projects—she should go far"; "He knows a great deal about the work"; "He gets the hang of problems more quickly than his immediate peers"; "I'm sure he has the potential to work at a higher stratum, but we just don't have the kind of work available that he's interested in."

Or, in the opposite vein, the comments run thus: "He seemed to be ready for promotion, so we gave him a temporary opportunity in a higher stratum role for which he had all the knowledge you could want, but he couldn't make it"; "In order to get him an advance to which we thought he was entitled, we got him into a technical role for which he had outstanding technical qualifications, but he just seemed to be unable to deal with the complexities of the problem"; "She has been with us for many years now, but I just don't think she's ready for any roles at the next stratum up." And so it goes.

We do get a clear sense of a common underlying understanding that some people we know have greater capability than ourselves, and others whom we know have lesser capability. And it is no new finding that immediate managers and managers-once-removed (MoRs) do know enough about immediate subordinates and subordinates-once-removed (SoRs) to judge their potential with considerable accuracy in relation to specific transfers, projects, or promotion possibilities.

Our hypothesis is that these judgments are based upon a sensing of the complexity of mental processing of people whom we know. We can sense it when another person is using higher or lower complexity processes than ourselves—for we feel encompassed by their thinking or that we encompass theirs. And in the case of individuals with whom we work, we can, and do, make fairly sharp judgments of where they are relative to ourselves.

The Importance of a Common Frame of Reference

The problem in research of this kind has been that no one has been able to pin down judgments of capability in well-articulated language. What has been lacking is a systematically constructed and defined conceptual scheme that can give shareable and communicable meaning to what is being judged. The first step toward overcoming that lack was the discovery by Jaques during the 1950s[1] of the general structure of stratification of the managerial hierarchical organization system. It is that template that has provided a language for individuals and their managers in companies that are requisitely organized, with which to articulate their judgments of level of capability in a manner comprehensible to others working in the same system or who understand it; that is to say, the language of the stratum (with its specific level of work range) at which an individual is judged to have the potential to work.

Work in managerial hierarchies is, of course, far from the only kind of work. There are many kinds of work, such as partnerships and elected political representatives, that are not organized as managerial hierarchies.

---

1. First published in Brown and Jaques (1965) *Glacier Project Papers*.

But the managerial hierarchy turned out to be an especially fruitful field of study because of the way its structure mirrors the structure of the categories of mental processing. By looking into the managerial hierarchy, the hierarchy of mental processing categories was there to be seen.

This assumption of the possible relationship between managerial strata and categories of complexity of mental processing was actually formulated by Jaques in the early 1960s and published in the following terms in 1965:

> The notion that there might be changes in the nature of capacity which accompany increases in the quantity or level of capacity came from the observation of executive hierarchies, in particular, the emergence of new managerial strata at given levels of work as measured in time-span. Consideration of this phenomenon suggests the hypothesis that these executive strata might correspond to differences in the levels of abstraction which have to be employed in order to make it possible for managerial leadership and authority to be exercised.
>
> If this hypothesis is valid, it would mean that we could expect to find that a manager well-established in his role would be working at an identifiably different level of abstraction from one of his subordinates well established in his own role one stratum below the manager's. Or looked at in terms of progression, a person would be perceived as becoming ready for promotion to the next higher stratum as he or she began to be able to apply a higher level of abstraction in his or her work.[2]

We suggest that our findings, twenty-five years later, confirmed this hypothesis. In order to get to this point it has been necessary to achieve an objectively definable set of types of mental processing and orders of information complexity. That has taken many years of continued refinement, reformulation, and redefinition of concepts, as can be seen by comparing the initial concepts formulated in 1964 with the present schema.[3] But there is another related outcome that is of some interest. Although this work started with the managerial hierarchy, the derived

---

2. *ibid.*
3. See appendix B for copy of relevant Glacier Metal Company memorandum.

findings about human capability are not confined to that type of organization alone. They apply to any and all kinds of mental processing in relation to any and all kinds of work; for as we have shown, the processing is independent of subject matter. We shall briefly illustrate this point in chapter 8 (pages 116–118) in connection with the issue of how the potential capability of candidates for elected political office shows up in political campaigning and subsequently in office. This argument implies that category of mental processing is an expression of the complexity of the total mental structure of the human being engaged in goal-directed behavior; that is to say, the human being at work.

Could These Mental Processes be Faked?

If our level of potential capability does show in the most complex category of mental processing we can use, might it not be possible for us to learn and to practice the use of more complex mental processes and thus to give a false impression of our potential capability? The answer to this question is no, for at least the following reasons.

First, it is unlikely to be possible to teach and rehearse a person to use a higher category of complexity of mental processing than their own natural maximum, in an unprepared and unrehearsed discussion. For in order to do so, that person would have to be occupied simultaneously with the hard work of formulating and stating arguments, and with thinking about how to put those arguments in the form of more complex mental processes.

We have found that not only is it not possible to argue spontaneously and freely at a level above one's level of current mental complexity, but also that it is not even possible to sustain a rehearsed argument at such a level. To try to do so is to experience information overload, with ensuing confusion and mental blocking.[4] In contrast, however, it is easy to use mental processes at a lower level than one's maximum. We do it all the time, for example, when engaged in discussion or arguing about some matter in which one is simply not interested and wishes to get away from with the least amount of effort possible.

---

4. Isaac and O'Connor demonstrated precisely this phenomenon experimentally in their study of truth tables as a formal device in the analysis of human actions.

This finding need not be surprising. It is merely that by withdrawal of interest and engrossment in a discussion, the level of complexity of one's mode of argument drops. But to take on a grossly intensified interest cannot enable you to do what you do not have the innate capability to do. It is much like lifting a weight: a light weight requires little effort, and it is easy to reduce effort to match it, but it is not possible by any degree of enthusiasm to go above one's maximum potential.

In short, if a person by training and rehearsal could learn how to use a more complex category of mental processing consistently and spontaneously in unrehearsed discussion and argument, it would not be fake, it would be real. And that would turn the question into one we have already raised; namely, is it possible by training or other process to help a person to increase his or her current potential capability? That question we have already commented upon, but will return to in the next chapter.

The Mental Processes And Modern Logic

We have recently sorted out a one-to-one relationship between the four mental processes and modern n-valued logic as represented in truth table connectives. The coincidence between the four processes and the four logical relationships is so perfect that there can be little doubt that the logicians have constructed the basic logical relationships as an intuitive response to the basic mental processes, and as an expression of these processes, in the same way that George Boole believed that the parallels between his class calculus and ordinary algebra were due to their common source in a "higher logic," the laws of thought.[5] Those who are familiar with computer sorting processes will recognize them as the four methods of sorting; namely, or-or; and-and; if-then-then; and, if-and-only-if.

The four logical or reasoning processes comprise two non-conditional processes: *or-* (vel, v), (disjunctive); *and-* (ut, ∧), (conjunctive); and two conditional processes, *if-then-then* (conditional, →); and *if-and-only-if*

---

5. Another connection has also occurred to us that is very likely a consequence of the four methods of mental processing; namely, the construction of the four major number scales—nominal, ordinal, interval, and ratio. This possible connection is discussed on page 105.

(bi-conditional, if $\rightleftarrows$), and have been set out in truth tables in the following form:

Figure 5.1
Truth Tables

p q	p ∨ q	p ∧ q	p →q	p ⇄q
T T	T	T	T	T
T F	T	F	F	F
F T	T	F	T	F
F F	F	F	T	T

These tables are to be read, for example, that *if* it is true that both p and q are true, *then* it is true that p *or* q is true, that p *and* q are true, that *if* p is true, *then* q is true, and that *if-and-only-if* p is true *then* q is true, and so on across each horizontal line.

Recognizing this possible relationship between the four mental processes and truth table logic also solved another problem for us. We have been aware that we had not had a satisfying term to refer to what we had called declarative and cumulative processing. We knew that they were significantly not serial, and so we referred to them, uncomfortably, as the two "plain" or "non serial" processes, recognizing that this ambiguous language reflected an insufficiently clear conceptualization. We can now recognize these two processes—in their clarified status as "or-or," and "and-and"—as the two non-conditional processes. By the same token, we can now recognize what we have termed the two "serial" processes—"serial" and "parallel"—as "conditional processing."

The following are the connections that we believe are self evident between the four mental processes and the four logical relationships.

Declarative processing and the disjunctive, non-conditional "or" (vel, v): The making of this connection has enabled us to sharpen our formulation of declarative processing. It is that type of processing not only in which no connections are made between the reasons for a particular conclusion, but in which the reasons are given in terms of declarative statements to the effect that "the reason could be p, or it might be q or then again it might be r." That formula was used some years ago at CRA (the Australian mining company) in a descriptive account of Stratum I work as follows: work in which an operator is given a prescribed operating layout to be followed, and if and when he or she runs up against a problem that lies outside the layout, then he or she is given alternative actions p *or* q *or* r to try, and if none works, then to go to see the first-line manager, and find out what to do. This formulation appears on page pair 24 of *Requisite Organization*.[6]

The notion of the or-or disjunctive non-conditional relationship thus gives a more pointed or expressive explanation to the processing we have been describing as the "declarative process."

Cumulative processing and the conjunctive non-conditional "and" (ut, ∧): Here again, we experience a further sharpening of the mental processing we have called cumulative. By cumulative we have referred to the non-serial accumulation of facts with explicitly stated connections between them. What we did not recognize, however, was that non-serial accumulation of related facts is limited to the conjunctive "and," and in fact, all our examples are of the same type; namely, "this, and this, along with this, all taken together, lead to the conclusion that . . . ." Our teaching has also been in this vein, as is the formulation on page pair 25 of *Requisite Organization*[7] in which the term "diagnostic accumulation" was used.

Serial processing and the conditional if-then (→): Now we turn to the translation of serial processing into conditional (if-then) processing. What we have described as serial, in the sense of "chains of two or more cause-and-effect connections, with the consequences of each connection leading into the next", is remarkably simplified when seen as chains of if-then (conditional) relationships; i.e., if p then q, if q then r, and so on.

The conditional "if-then" relationship also gives a more interesting and explanatory formulation of the description of Stratum III task complexity in terms of alternative paths (*Requisite Organization*, page pair 26). The construction of pathways is a succession of if-then steps; namely, "If I did this, then I could do that, and if I could do that, then I could do this other" and so on.

Parallel processing and the bi-conditional if-and-only-if (⇄) relationship: We defined parallel processing (*Requisite Organization*, page pair 27) as "two or more serial processes related to each other in parallel." A more precise definition is to see them as two or more "if-then" processes, one

---

6. Jaques (1989) *Requisite Organization*.
7. *ibid.*

dependent upon the other (i.e., bi-conditional); that is to say, given a certain condition p, then a conclusion q is warranted, given q, then r is warranted, etc., but *if-and-only-if* there is another related if-then condition c that leads on to d, d that leads on to e, or a number of such related if-then conditions. It is this relationship between two or more if-then propositions that gives the sense of parallel processing.

This processing is described in *Requisite Organization* (page pair 27) in the following terms for Stratum IV task complexity. "In short: At Stratum IV you have to parallel process several interacting projects, pacing them in relation to one another in resourcing and in time. You must make trade-offs between tasks in order to maintain progress along the composite route to the goal."

Because of the crispness and fullness of the logic language, we shall be using it in the future. Here in summary are the old and the new.

Figure 5.2
Summary of Terms

OLD TERMS			NEW TERMS	
non-serial	⎰ declarative	disjunctive	⎰ or-or: p or q or r	
plain	⎱ cumulative	conjunctive	⎱ and-and: p and q and r	
serial	⎰ serial	conditional	⎰ if-then-then: if p then q, if q then r	
	⎱ parallel	bi-conditional	⎱ if-and-only-if: if p then q, but if-and-only if r then s	

The remaining question, of course, is whether or not this development in terminology might significantly have changed the course of our study and the results. We have carefully checked over the transcripts to discover whether such an effect might have happened. The only effect, and a very desirable one, is that we have found that the new formulation has helped us to focus our attention more sharply on the material. We have found, in addition, that it is easier to teach the nature of the four processes with the help of the new language than it has been by using the old language. The clearer and more exact formulation of the concepts has made them more readily accessible for communicating and understanding.

PART III

Some Practical Implications

6

Current Applied Capability (CAC)

In concentrating thus far upon our research study, we have inevitably focused upon current potential capability (CPC), the highest complexity of mental processing (CMP) currently available to the individual within his or her unique maturational process. We propose in the next three chapters to widen our discussion, and to consider first, the operation of current applied capability (CAC), second, the question of the maturation of potential capability, and third, a number of wider ranging practical implications of our approach to human capability.

In chapter 2, we defined current applied capability (CAC) as the level of capability a person is actually exercising at a particular time in carrying out specific tasks. It is the source of his or her personal effectiveness in whatever work he or she might happen to be doing. Current applied capability (CAC) is determined not only by that person's complexity of mental processing (CMP) but also by how much he or she values (V) (is committed to) that specific work, the level of his or her experience and skilled knowledge (K/S) for carrying it out, and freedom from dysfunctional personal characteristics (-T). The level of applied capability can never be higher than a person's current complexity of mental processing (CMP), and will usually be more or less lower. The difference will be in whatever shortfall there might be with respect to V and K/S for the work: low commitment can reduce the amount of potential that is expressed; low K/S and (-T) can reduce the effectiveness of its expression.

Thus, on the one hand, current potential capability is a dynamic constant, modified only by continuous maturation. On the other hand, however, a person's current applied capability (CAC), and therefore his or her immediate personal effectiveness, may vary substantially for different kinds of work. One's CAC may be high, for example, for financial work, but low for production management; or high for writing poetry, but low for being a chef; or high for selling, but low for design engineering. No one is omnicompetent, omniscient, or equally interested and committed to everything.

Elements in Applied Capability
Commitment to Type of Work (V)

We are here using commitment in the sense of how much a person values doing the work; not in the generic sense of ethics and moral values, but rather in the more specific sense of how much individuals value the particular types of work which they are actually doing at a particular time. It will be readily apparent that the more that individuals value the work they are doing, the more likely it will be that they will maintain the attempt to apply their full potential. The less the work is valued, the less will be the commitment to muster the full potential.

There are many ways in which the value of a given role in general, or particular tasks within a role, can fall below the commitment level necessary for the full exercise of our potential. Thus, for example, there is the simple case of sheer lack of interest in work that one might not choose to do, but which social or economic circumstances might force one to do, as for example, with high levels of unemployment; or where individuals do not have the necessary skilled knowledge for the work that they would be interested in and for which they did have the necessary level of potential capability; or where there is a sharp divergence of values between employer and employed.

Then there are personal, family, and related issues that may distract people, so that they cannot focus adequately upon their work. Individuals know about such problems—so do their managers. Among these issues are individual problems, ranging from distracting physical disabilities and illnesses, to acute or chronic depression and other types of distracting psychological disturbances.

But perhaps the most common source of eroding of value and commitment in work are the myriad kinds of non-requisite organizations that are to be found almost everywhere in the managerial employment systems in which the vast majority of people work. These include: having a manager who is not sufficiently higher in capability than the subordinate, because the organization has too many layers or because of poor appointments and promotions; inadequate managerial leadership processes; poor task assignment; unclear accountability and authority in working relationships; defective and unfair compensation systems; and so on and on. Everyone will be familiar enough with just how far it is possible for such circumstances to cause individuals to lose their sense of value for their work, and how far below their potential capability it is possible for their applied capability to be reduced as a result. How to overcome these problems, commonly referred to as lack of motivation, depends upon the nature of the problem.

Lack of opportunity because of unemployment or because of lack of education and training, are the issues we shall address at the end of chapter 8, in terms of the basic requirements of a decent society. Personal difficulties of individuals are matters for those individuals to seek help for, but it is important that employment organizations should have sound policies with respect to reasonable opportunities for individuals to have time off for serious endeavors to sort out or to overcome such difficulties.

When it comes to apathy resulting from the widespread adverse impact upon people of non-requisitely organized employment organizations, we have a chronic problem in modern society that urgently needs to be addressed. Over 90% of the working population in countries like the United States and England do their work by employment for a wage or salary in such organizations. The cumulative toll in poor morale is vastly underestimated, or even more seriously, denied. It is a public health problem of the first magnitude.

What needs to be done to eliminate this last problem is to achieve requisite organization in our managerial employment systems, including sound organizational structuring, requisite managerial leadership practices, and role filling in which individual capability matches the complexity of roles, all combined to ensure effective managerial leadership and individual opportunity, at all levels. It has been demonstrated that full-scale requisite organization almost totally banishes apathy, and allows for full release of capability. Individuals can get deep satisfaction out of their work and the organizations prosper. The means now exist for doing so.[1]

The difficulty is that companies are widely committed to the use of the most superficial fads to try to improve their organizations. They are supported almost universally through the creation of such fads by academic experts, and by assistance from managerial consultants in implementing them. It is our hope that the clarification of the nature of potential capability and of the importance of each individual's valuing of specific kinds of work as requirements for getting full use of individual applied capability, will contribute to the spreading of a deeper and more serious approach to overcoming this degrading social problem.

Elements in Applied Capability
Skilled Knowledge (K/S)

Knowledge affects our applied capability in work differently from the effect of the intensity of our valuing of the work and our commitment to doing it. The degree to which we value the work influences the degree to which we invest our full potential capability, thereby influencing our personal effectiveness and level of applied capability. Our skilled knowledge in relation to particular tasks affects our applied capability by influencing the effectiveness with which we can apply the potential capability that we are committing to the work. The greater the relevant knowledge, the greater our effectiveness will be.

Skilled knowledge has to do with tools with which to do the work. It comprises the articulated information about the work that we have accumulated through education, training, and experience. It includes the facts and procedures and the rules and regulations that we apply in problem solving, and the language in which these facts and procedures are stated. By skill we refer to our ability to use the knowledge and the procedures of which we have knowledge automatically. These procedures may call for the manual and bodily skills required, for example, in manual operator roles, in surgery, in sports, in parachute jumping; or they may be mental procedures—as in carrying out accountancy or purchasing or research or design procedures or in exercising managerial leadership

---

1. See Jaques (1989) *Requisite Organization*, and Jaques and Clement (1991) *Executive Leadership*.

processes. It may also be noted that the effectiveness of application of motor skills can be strongly influenced by complexity of mental processing, as for example, in high level professional sports (boxing, tennis, football, etc.) or in surgical skills.

Knowledge sets the framework for goal-directed problem-solving behavior. Bits and pieces of knowledge judged to be relevant are pulled out of our mental storehouse, are put together like a jigsaw puzzle, and are formed into conduits or channels within which our mental processing flows. We can thus use our available knowledge to focus our attention, to focus our efforts, and to direct our behavior towards the goal we are seeking to reach. To put the same proposition in psychoanalytical terms, knowledge is the expression of our conscious mental functioning (and our available pre- conscious functions), which sets the context for our unconscious mental processes (used here in the sense of our ordinary mental flows with their innate complexity, rather than of irrationality).

It will be apparent that knowledge will become increasingly valuable as its use becomes increasingly skilled. Skill is achieved by practice through training and through experience. Problem solving can be markedly simplified through the development of procedures, rules, and regulations that people can be taught to use in a skilled way. It is this kind of simplification that allows what had been complex tasks to be less so and therefore to be delegated to lower levels in managerial employment systems—the basis of our mass production system.

The way in which the possession of relevant skilled knowledge helps to channel our mental process flow, and thus to organize our behavior, is readily seen if we contrast it with our behavior in dealing with unfamiliar problems under unfamiliar circumstances. In the latter case we are reduced to much trial and error as we attempt to get a focus on what needs to be done, and to bring into play and test what we do know that might prove to be relevant.

The centerpiece of all skilled knowledge is our knowledge of our language, or better, of more than one language. Any extension of our vocabulary is an extension of our knowledge. The ability to read and write our language is a major leap forward in knowledge, especially when these abilities become skilled knowledge; i.e., we can read and write without thinking about the ability to do so and can therefore focus on the content.

The fact that our language is part of our knowledge, and thus plays a part in channeling and directing our mental process flows so as to focus upon reaching intended goals, is the prime reason why precision and unequivocality are so important in technical language, and above all, in scientific language. In our field of organizational development, the slovenly use of language, and the widespread pooh-poohing of the need for precision, is a major handicap. For example, it is impossible to direct constructive mental effort for the problem of effective managerial training if you do not have a precise definition of the concept of manager with which to direct your attention to what you are trying to do—and, indeed, to communicate this direction to others with whom you may be trying to work.

Much of our knowledge is constitutionally innate. We come into the world with a substantial endowment of potential knowledge. As Bion[2] has put it, we arrive with a complex panoply of preconceptions seeking their realization and formulation as conceptions—that is to say, as knowledge. As child analysis has shown, for example, not only does the infant have a primitive knowledge of a breast and of how to direct a complex set of behaviors towards the breast, but as Chomsky has demonstrated, we have a full-scale innate underpinning for language and grammar. And then throughout life, knowledge and skilled knowledge pile up by learning, training, and experience. Potential capability, it will be obvious, plays a limiting role on this process of acquisition of knowledge. For, if information is more complex than the complexity of mental processing of the individual, then the knowledge cannot be acquired.

One of the ways in which we may increase our applied capability is by increasing our skilled knowledge by discovering better ways of doing the work we have chosen or have been given to do. Developing such knowledge is, for example, one of the main ways in which operators on piecework bonus systems increase their earnings. They do so, not so much by moving faster and faster, but rather by working smarter. That is to say, on the one hand they become increasingly skilled, and on the other hand they develop special ways of doing things, they grow new knowledge for themselves, and thereby increase their applied capability.

Knowledge comprises both the knowledge of the world we accumulate through experience, and the knowledge we learn whether from books,

---

2. Bion (1962) *Learning from Experience.*

or teachers, or others. It includes not only knowledge of the material, social, and economic worlds, but also knowledge of human nature and behavior.

This last point contains a major issue about knowledge; namely, that it may be more or less accurate or valid. Indeed, it may range from accurate and therefore efficient, to inaccurate or downright misleading. The question of how we test the validity of our knowledge would take us eventually into nothing less than the questions of scientific testing and the nature of knowledge and reality, questions we shall not presume to address. We shall leave ourselves with a pragmatic approach to that crude everyday conception of the skilled knowledge that we all possess with respect to making as full use as possible of our potential capability as we work at specific problems in what we call the real world.

Elements in Applied Capability
Temperamental Characteristics (-T)

A last question that must be considered is that of the role in applied capability of so-called personality or enduring temperamental characteristics; such qualities as initiative, aggressiveness, flexibility, emotional warmth, optimism, curiosity, reliability, caring, and many others, plus their opposites. Such factors affect applied capability indirectly or directly. The indirect effect occurs via the impact of these enduring personal characteristics upon the development of our values, the values that in turn determine what we choose to do and that affect our intensity of commitment in different circumstances.

The direct effect occurs through the immediate impact of the negative or inhibiting degrees of pessimism, or lassitude, or unreliability, or social abrasiveness, and so on, that will prevent us from applying our full potential in particular circumstances.

Our proposition is that in the absence of negative disruptive personal characteristics, and in work which we value and to which we can therefore happily commit our potential, there are no specific personal characteristics or patterns of characteristics that it is necessary to have in specially high degree for given types of work. We all possess the same full range of characteristics (whatever the classifications of these characteristics we might use—and there are many such classifications), and there are infinite possible combinations or profiles of degrees of these characteristics that may be effective. Thus, despite what many people would say, even leadership capability does not call for specially high degrees of charisma, or initiative, or sociability. The outstanding feature of successful political, or military, or managerial leaders, for example, is the enormously wide range of patterns of higher and lesser degrees of their various personal qualities; in short, the most striking feature is just how much they vary as people, rather than fitting into a few neat combinations of traits.

Our experience has been that it is very often the case that when people describe some particular personality qualities to explain that someone has shown outstanding capability in a role, they are unwittingly reacting to the fact that that person possesses a level of capability greater than that required by the ordinarily expected level of work in the role. Thus, for example, an unusually inspiring teacher said to have emotional warmth, or a highly effective political leader said to be highly flexible, or a principal who transforms a school from mediocrity to excellence by virtue of a strong personal strain of determination, are most likely to be so outstanding because of levels of complexity of mental processing (CMP), commitment and skilled knowledge, that enable them to function at unusually high levels. Others, with different patterns of personality qualities, but with the same levels of applied capability, would do just as well.

In our formula for applied capability, therefore, we have provided for personality-influenced values in terms of value and commitment (V) and any direct impact of disruptive or negative temperamental characteristics as "minus T" (-T). Hence:

Figure 6.1
Formula for Current Applied Capability

CAC	= f	CMP	V	K/S	(-T)
Current	is a	Complexity	Value and	Skilled	Minus T
Applied	function	of Mental	commitment	Knowledge	(if any)
Capability	of	Processing	to the task		inhibits

7

Maturation of Potential Capability

Our experience has been that there is a cluster of questions that are repeatedly raised with respect to our findings. For example, how does a person's current potential capability get to be what it is? How does it develop? Can it be enhanced by education and training or by special opportunity? Can it be inhibited by lack of opportunity because of gender, color, race, or ethnic background? Is its growth and development predictable? These questions are of such importance in connection with our current study that this report would not be complete were we not to address them. In order to address them, however, we shall have to refer to other, related studies.

Let us first establish a clear distinction between the concepts of development and maturation. We shall use development to refer in a general way to change through time, as for example, in speaking about a person's emotional development, or the development of a professional practice, the eventual outcome of which cannot be foreseen at the beginning. The term maturation, however, we shall use rigorously in the more limited sense of one special kind of development; namely, a natural unfolding built into the growing organism, moving towards an end-point that is knowable from the beginning and therefore is predictable, i.e., the biological maturation of a human being from the formed fetus with its cephalic protrusion and limb buds to the fully developed adult.

Maturation processes are often incorrectly thought about as produced solely by the nature of the organism rather than by the environment, the result of nature rather than nurture. In fact, they are a function of both. Organisms exist only in their environment and are always influenced by environmental forces. What is special about maturation processes is that they unfold in accord with a constitutionally predetermined pattern so long as the organism lives in an ordinarily challenging environment and does not encounter any exceptional environmental deprivation in early life. That is to say, the exigencies of everyday environmental conditions and life experiences are sufficient for maturation to occur in the absence of severely deleterious conditions. If severely deleterious conditions do not occur, the predictable maturation process will unfold. If such conditions do occur, the maturation will be disturbed and a crippled or handicapped organism will result. Such a go-no-go situation is quite different from the meaning of organism-environment interaction in non-maturational development, as, for example, in the development of particular kinds of values or of skilled knowledge, in which a wide range of unpredictable directions of development may occur depending upon the environmental circumstances that may arise.

To return to the question, then, of whether the potential capability of individuals merely develops in one way or another in accord with specific environmental circumstances and opportunities, or whether it is a true maturation process, we shall now present evidence, accumulated over the past thirty-five years, that it is a very hardy maturational process. The ordinary everyday world brings more than enough opportunity for individuals to exercise their full potential capability—possibly in school or at work, but if not, then most certainly in coping with the exigencies of life in family, in gangs, in the community, and in all the other institutions and social relationships that interweave to create the circumstances and the daily problems of the lives we lead.

In short, the evidence we shall describe favors the conclusion that each person's potential capability matures in a predictable way throughout life from childhood to old age, fed by having to cope with the exigencies of everyday life. This maturation process is unlikely to be able to be speeded up or enhanced by special educational procedures or occupational opportunities, nor impeded by the less favorable social, educational, and occupational opportunities faced by many minorities, since such opportunities or their absence are far less important for individual maturation in *potential* capability than the problems that have to be solved in living our everyday lives.

A Multi-Track Theory of Maturation of Potential Capability

The accompanying chart (figure 7.1) shows the patterns of maturation of potential capability, as developed by one of us (Jaques) over the past thirty-five years.

Figure 7.1
Time Horizon Progression Array

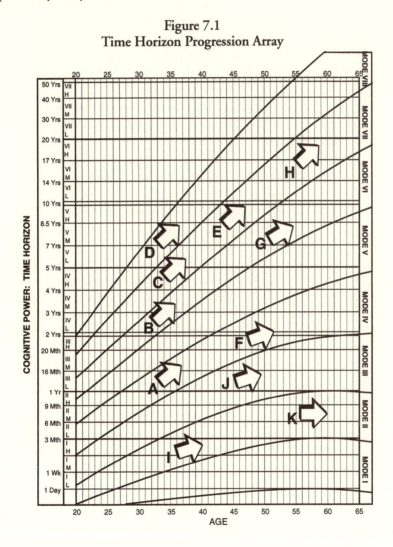

It may be noted that our conception of maturation of potential capability differs strikingly from the established models of psychological development in two very important respects. The first respect is that the Jaques model of maturation extends from childhood to old age. Most developmental studies such as those of Piaget and Kohlberg have made developmental psychology synonymous with child psychology: the studies span infancy to adolescence, and not much later. By the same token studies of IQ posit that "intelligence" matures fully by 16 to 18 years of age. But of course IQ is technically defined as that which is measured by intelligence tests—a circular definition indeed. Developmental models such as those of Levinson[1] and Kegan[2] deal with the whole of the life cycle. But to the extent that they are maturational models, the maturational component would appear to be due rather more to the impact of the maturation of mental complexity on a person's social growth than upon the maturation of some innate awareness of self and others.

The second significant difference from current psychological development theory concerns the assumptions about the number of development tracks. It has been assumed by Piaget and others that there is only one development track along which everyone progresses: people may progress more or less quickly along this track, or end up progressing farther or less far along it, but there is just one pathway and everyone is crowded onto it. By contrast, Jaques discovered empirically the existence of more than a dozen clearly bounded maturation pathways, or bands, each with its own specific and definable end point. It is these bands which are set out on the chart in figure 7.1.

The curved bands in figure 7.1 set out what studies since 1958 have shown to be the broad bands within which individuals mature in their ability to handle complexity in working at problems—the natural bands of maturation of mental complexity. Thus if you have a person, A, 30 years of age and with a current potential working-capacity of top grade Stratum II, he or she is likely to have the potential to move through Stratum III in about 15 years, and to move into a Stratum IV role at about 45 years of age. Or a person, B, 29 years of age recently promoted into Stratum IV and with the potential to work in the bottom grade of

---

1. Levinson (1978) *The Seasons of a Man's Life.*
2. Kegan (1982) *The Emerging Self.*

Stratum IV (2- to 3-year time-span), is likely to have the potential to move into Stratum V at about age 40, and then to move through Stratum V in about 15 years.

In figure 7.1, B, C, D, and E indicate the levels of work potential corporate executives should be capable of handling between the ages of 30 to 40 years. Their native working capacity (CPC) and time horizons have matured to these points and achieving positions at these levels allow them to fully use this capacity.

These maturation bands were first deduced from the discovery of a regular pattern of progression of the real earnings of individuals over periods of years, like the lines of force you can see in iron filings on the surface of a sheet of paper with a bar magnet underneath. Their validity has been established in studies tracking the careers of individuals for periods of up to thirty years.

Jaques followed the careers of 196 individuals for periods of eighteen to thirty years. Among the data he was able to gather were judgments on the occasions when each individual felt that he or she had had an employment role whose work was "just right" in the sense of giving them the opportunity to use their full potential capability in their work. He was also able to obtain the time-span of their roles at those times.

Results: the data were analyzed and plotted by T. Kohler at UCLA, in terms of each person's "comfort curve"; that is to say, the time-spans described above for each person were plotted as a curve on the progression data sheets.[3] The comfort curves followed within the progression bands in all cases but two in which there were slight deviations, supporting the proposition that maturation of potential capability follows predictable patterns. Examples of the types of progression curves obtained are shown in figure 7.2.

In follow-up studies, Gillian Stamp has shown the maturation bands to be accurate predictors of future potential.[4] Using a clinical method she developed for evaluating complexity of mental processing, she obtained a .89 correlation between the working potential of individuals as shown in their work, and as predicted by extrapolation along the progression bands from her evaluations of potential capability six to fourteen years earlier.

---

3. Kohler (1986) Unpublished analysis of follow-up data collected by Jaques.
4. Stamp (1988) "Longitudinal Research into Methods of Assessing Managerial Potential."

Her studies have ranged from industrially developed western cultures to less developed countries with little or no school education in the Western sense. The patterns of maturation of time-horizon and cognitive power are the same. We would appear to be dealing with a deeply in-built human characteristic.

Two significant features of these maturation bands can be noted. The higher a person's potential capability, the faster is the rate of maturation and the later in life it continues. The higher capability individuals are still growing in potential capability long after normal retirement age.

Figure 7.2
Comfort Curves

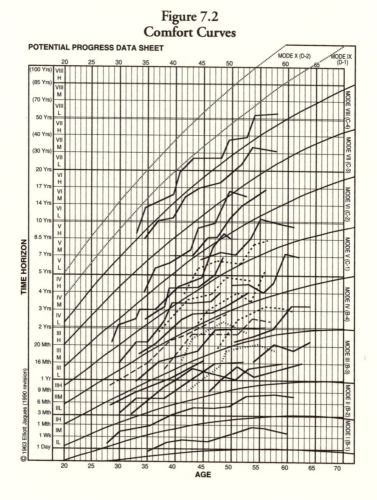

Jaques & Cason

The hypothesis is that each person has a constitutionally established maximum future potential capability and matures at a predictable rate from infancy to old age to reach that full potential. The age at which full potential is reached varies with the level of potential. The higher the level of a person's full potential, the later in life will that potential continue to mature and the final maximum level be reached: the so-called mentally handicapped reach full maturity of potential in early adulthood; those with the potential to reach mental process categories B1 to B4 reach full maturity in late adulthood; and those with potential to move into categories at C1 and above will have died before they reach their absolute peak.

If this multi-track maturation hypothesis is valid, then it ought to be the case that a person's eventual mental process or mode should be observable at younger ages before full mental processing maturity. In fact, researchers, such as one of the authors, Cason, and Owen T. Jacobs have found that they are able to recognize the predictable level of full maturation (what we call mode) in subjects with great reliability. The problem is that no one has as yet been able to articulate precisely what it is that is being observed. It is like the recognition of current potential capability. Fairly reliable judgments have been made for nearly thirty years without anyone having been able until recently to identify and to articulate the mental processes whose existence we have now described reliably and validated in relation to judged potential in actual work. It can only be hoped that another thirty-year search will not be necessary in order to identify and to articulate just what it is that skilled observers are responding to when they judge the mental mode—the maximum future potential of individuals. It has much of the feeling of the search to identify and to articulate the double helix structure of DNA—and could have equally significant consequences.

Some possible features of mental processing mode can be offered. Higher mode people seem always to use more complex language—starting in childhood and experienced in "the bright sayings of bright children." Mode may also reveal itself in spicules of high complexity argument; that is to say, when a person, it would seem out of the blue, from time to time produces a brief and surprisingly complex idea in relation to a problem. And finally, individuals of a given mental mode seem to have a special understanding of individuals of equivalent mode but at different levels of current potential capability. Thus, for example, a senior executive at fully matured potential capability at category C3 (conceptual serial), and making full use of that potential in a Stratum VII role, may bring two graduate professionals up to assist him with work on a development project. Let us say that both of the graduates are currently at high B3 in potential, but that A is 25 years of age and Mode C3, whereas B is 33 years of age and Mode C1. The senior executive will find that A (the younger higher mode individual) will understand him much more fully than does B, and that once given a lead on what to do will respond much more imaginatively, even though A and B are at the same level of current potential capability at that time. This phenomenon is familiar enough. The only problem is to articulate how it works and that will call for continuing effort and study.

A Note on "Predestination"

Hypotheses of the kind we have outlined about potential capability and its development inevitably give rise to criticism on political grounds. They are held to be politically reactionary on racial grounds or of being neofeudal in the sense of putting individuals into fixed slots in life. These criticisms are incorrect, but they are of substantial importance and warrant comment. They relate to the ethical questions considered by the authors in the preface, and this commentary follows on from the argument pursued in that section.

It is gratifying to be able to report that the evidence obtained by ourselves and our colleagues is that individuals mature in mental complexity and in potential capability under the impact of the problems presented by everyday life, regardless of gender, race, color, ethnic, or social background, and regardless of whether those problems have had to be faced under the exigencies of privileged school learning or under the exigencies of survival in a setting of social and educational deprivation. Who is to say which is likely to provide the greater stimulus?

Let us emphasize that we are talking only about maturation of complexity of mental processing and the concomitant potential capability. We are not talking about the social and economic opportunity to exercise that potential capability in education or employment, or to gain the education, experience, orientation, or skilled knowledge needed to advance in our society. If these hypotheses about maturation turn out to be valid, it would mean that whether or not individuals have adequate social, educational, or occupational opportunities for developing particular psychological tools and orientation, their potential capability will mature nonetheless. If, however, they do not have the opportunity to learn and to develop the necessary knowledge, tools, and orientation for work that matches their capability, people will fall behind in their ability to compete in their societies. At the very least, they will be frustrated and fed up and feel unjustly treated because they do not have the chance to exercise their full potential capability in socially acceptable ways, and thereby to reap their fair share of the wealth of that society.

If the discrepancies between potential capability, on the one hand, and skilled knowledge and work opportunities, on the other, are great, most people will fall seriously behind in status and in achievement. Some will work zealously to overcome this disadvantage, and a few will become social reformers. But many others will become alienated and may instigate more or less violent social change. Or they may engage in anti-social or delinquent outlets in which to express their capability, ranging anywhere from criminal occupations to apparently mindless violence. It is precisely because maturation in potential capability occurs despite social and economic opportunity that social alienation and resentment can occur, led by those with the highest levels of underutilized potential. Any society, to be a decent society, must provide the opportunity for individuals to gain the skilled knowledge and values necessary for them to be able to use their potential to the full and must ensure the provision of fullest employment opportunities for all.[5]

Indeed, it is the prevailing viewpoint that educational and social opportunity are necessary for the maturation of a person's level of cognitive power that is more difficult to understand. For that view contains the implicit assumption that under generations of subjugation or social, educational, and economic deprivation, disadvantaged or subject peoples would have produced populations of intellectual morons. Human nature and the maturation of potential capability appear, fortunately, to be far more resilient than that. And, as we argued in the introduction, the existence in society of objective and shareable knowledge of each one's true potential capability would make it far more difficult to use judgments

---

5. Jaques (1982) *Free Enterprise, Fair Employment.*

of capability distorted by bias and prejudice to justify deprivation of opportunity to some groups.

Finally, we would repeat that the assessments of current potential capability that we have described are a very far cry from the world of IQ ratings. Our whole orientation is toward the performance of individuals in planning and carrying out goal-directed activities and, thus, in constructing their own worlds. This orientation has little relation to IQ and equivalent ratings which fail to separate individual potential capability from culturally dominated knowledge and values. Such ratings lean too heavily on culturally learned values and language and on ability to learn what is taught in schools, whether or not the individual has been to school or even liked that kind of learning.

In short, the concept of maturation of individual potential seems to some people to run counter to the democratic dream of opportunity for everyone to reach the very top (whatever that might mean). That this view is unwarranted is shown by two sets of findings; namely, the unrealistic beliefs that people have about what others might be striving for, and the realistic judgments we have of what we ourselves might be capable of achieving.

When it comes to others, some people are inclined to believe that everyone working at levels in the organization below them is trying to be on a par with them. They find it difficult to believe that people working below them could be satisfied to be where they are. This condescending attitude is wide of the mark with respect to the career hopes and expectations of all but the greedy and emotionally disturbed. And it is a disparagement of all work below you as being somehow inferior.

At the same time, *if we have been fortunate enough to be in work that matches our current potential,* it does not seem to occur to us to covet the work of those above us, at least not in the sense of really wanting to be in their shoes right now. Nor does it occur to us that those working above us might be looking down their noses at us in the same way that we do to those below.

When it comes to ourselves, however, we are not self-aggrandizing, not privately anyhow. Whatever the public show we might feel we have to put on, we do not seek to break ourselves by progressing above our potential capability. What we all really yearn for is to have work at a level consistent with our current potential and for progression to match our future potential, and for the chance to get the necessary education and training. *That is the true democratic dream.*

Some Speculations about Infant and Child Development

It obviously must be the case, from our findings thus far, that there are orders of information complexity both less complex and more complex than the two orders we have described. On the side of less complexity, there must be at least one other that relates to childhood. On the side of greater complexity, there must be at least one other order, and there is no reason to suppose that there is any inherent limitation on the number of orders there might be, just as the number of octaves in music could go up to very large numbers regardless of the fact that the human ear would be unable to hear them.

With regard to less complex information, we would assume first of all a probably closely related concrete or immediately perceived order of information complexity characteristic of children and of adults characterized as mentally handicapped to Piaget's four stages—see page 97. The nature of the information complexity is that specific and concrete objects must be at hand, or in mind, for the child to be able to use language and ideas in problem solving: that is to say, in dealing with toys, or clothing, or other objects, the child will have specific toys, or clothing, or objects in mind, either concretely at hand or to be referred to even though they may be in another place.[6] In other words, the information and language are directly tied to concrete objects-to-be-pointed-to, rather than to categories of objects as is the case with information and language in the world of second order ideas and language described in our research as B1 to B4.

In addition, however, the authors would hypothesize that there is a more primitive order of information complexity; namely, the gestural order of information that precedes the verbal stages of infant development. We shall refer to it as order AG; i.e., order A Gestural, in contrast to order AV, i.e., order A Verbal. We would postulate that Order AG exists during the first two years when infants communicate by reaching, grasping, grabbing,

---

6. Jaques (1986) "The Development of Intellectual Capability", *Journal of Applied Behavioral Science.*

gesturing, and pulling, accompanied by crying, uttering, and babbling. It is the pre-verbal period characterized in memory not by words but by what Melanie Klein has so vividly described as the memories-in-feeling that turn up in the psychoanalysis of young children.[7]

Our working hunch would be that the maturing infant progresses through the four basic patterns of mental processing, expressed in gesture, starting with category AG1, or category AG declarative, and proceeding to category AG4 or category AG parallel processing. The possible connection between this hunch and a reinterpretation of Piaget's pre-verbal sub-stages is discussed on page 99.

But let us leave this problematic hunch, and move to the stronger ground of childhood maturation through order of information complexity we shall call AV—A Verbal. Our hypothesis is that children mature through the four patterns of mental process as they grow toward adulthood, in the following manner. Declarative processing (category AV1) is the pattern of the infant, who makes assertions in physical behavior accompanied by primitive words (emerging from verbal grunts) as he or she relates to the objects of interest in the surrounding world. There is a gesturing and reaching towards this or that while grunting and mouthing and forming sounds into first words which are just there. The pressure towards verbal utterance can be seen in the coordination of mouth movements with hand movements as the infant reaches out to grab things.

The next stage (AV2) is that of sentence formation. It requires cumulative processing in the sense of the putting together and combining of ideas in order to put together the words that cumulatively form a sentence.

Then there is a third stage (AV3) in which the child moves on from cumulative to serial processing roughly from three to five years of age in children of very high potential (Modes C3 and C4) to from five to ten years of age in children at the lower end of the so-called normal range (Mode B1 and B2) and later still in the so-called mentally handicapped. The main feature of this stage is that a child behaves serially in the sense that it decides to carry out a simple project like re-arranging a doll's house, or making a hideaway in the garden, thinks up a plan of action, and is determined to

---

7. Klein (1975) *Narrative of a Child Analysis, Collected Writings, The Psychoanalysis of Children.*

carry it out. If interrupted and prevented from carrying out its plan, the child may have a temper tantrum. For just like any serial processing, the individual has created a plan of action, is sure of what he or she must do, and is determined to do it. Any break in the serial process is resented, and the phase in childhood is characterized by temper tantrums.

The third, serial state is followed by a fourth, parallel processing stage, in which the temper tantrums are replaced by a phase of strong socialization in which the individual can now understand not only the serial pathway which he or she is intent on following, but can also take into account the pathways that others might be wishing to follow. Conflicting goals and pathways can be reflected upon in parallel, and related to each other with the ability to modify one's own goals and pathways to adjust appropriately to the plans and actions of others, without having to hang on rigidly to the direction one has set.

The fourth stage lasts from roughly five to ten years of age in high mode children (Modes VII and VIII) and from ten to twenty years of age in youngsters in Modes I and II. This fourth stage is the highest level of development of capability in adulthood in so-called mentally handicapped individuals.

The succeeding stage of maturation is to mental processing cat. B1. This stage will be reached around age seven to ten by the high mode children, and not till about age 20 by the Mode B1 and B2 children. This proposition could well explain the need for multiple levels of NCOs in military combat organizations: most of the private soldiers will be between 18 and 20 years of age, and most of this age group will have matured only to A4 category of mental processing. Under the exigencies of the complexity, the rapid movement and the great noise and confusion of the battlefield, the concrete orientation of such soldiers will not suffice to keep themselves organized. The soldiers have to be grouped into teams of four and squads of eight to twelve, each with an NCO, at cat. B1 (Stratum I) capability, to help them to keep themselves under control.

These hypotheses about the maturation of complexity of mental processing in childhood are summarized in a rough extrapolation of the adult mental process maturation bands back into childhood as shown in figure 7.3. This chart is a very rough construction indeed. We started with the assumption that it must follow the shape of a sigmoid biological growth curve. We then took span of attention data from the child

Figure 7.3
Preliminary Hypothesis of Maturation of Complexity of Mental Processing (Potential Capability) from Infancy to Old Age

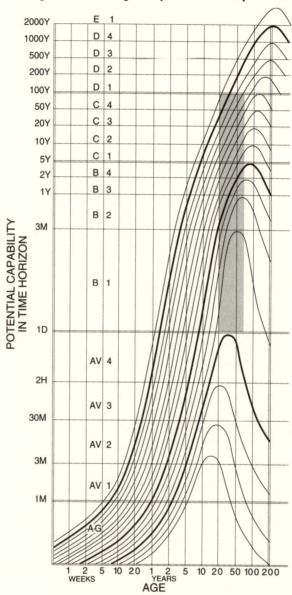

Jaques & Cason

development field, and used them to make assumptions about ranges of time horizons in the first twelve months of life. Working in this crude manner, we used other data from the field of mental handicap development in placing the peaks of the lower level development curves. We also have collected random bits of data about individual children between two years and fifteen years of age, and placed them on the chart. We then joined all these data to the tail end of the curves in the shadowed column, which represents the progression data sheet plotted with age on a logarithmic rather than an arithmetic scale. We believe that this construction will turn out to be a useful first approximation to the patterns of maturation of mental complexity throughout life.

The curves do, for example, predict that if Mozart was a genius at Mode D1 to D4 level of complexity, then he would have been at B3 level of mental complexity between five and ten years of age, and that would have been sufficient for composing the first symphony that he produced at that time. They have also been constructed so that the average population, in Mode B2, moves across the AG/AV boundary, and thus begins full speech at about 18 months of age. Moving to the left across this boundary line, the prediction would be that speech begins to show during the second six months in very high potential babies, and even earlier in genius. The chart is full of interesting predictive possibilities, all testable, and all to be tested in due course.

Comparison with Piaget's Stages

Our findings call for comparison with Piaget's formulation of his four stages. There are a number of similarities and some important differences. The clearest and most systematic formulation of his theory of stages is presented in his book *Logic and Psychology*,[8] and we will use that text for our comparison, along with his *The Origins of Intelligence in Children*[9] in connection with his concept of sub-stages.

The first similarity lies in the assumption of discontinuous stages. Piaget is inclined to suppose a more gentle evolutionary movement from one stage to another than our evidence would suggest. But, nevertheless,

---

8. Piaget (1957) *Logic and Psychology.*
9. Piaget (1952) *The Origins of Intelligence in Children.*

he is clear about the fact of there being substantial qualitative changes that occur. The second similarity lies in the fact that he believes that strong maturational forces are at work, even though he allows for a greater impact of experience and learning than we would, an emphasis that derives from his inclusion of knowledge in his analysis of stages as well as change in mental processes.

A third similarity lies in the use that he makes of connectives in symbolic logic. In particular he refers his operational stage of the child's maturation to the point where it can utilize all sixteen operations contained in the truth table matrix (see figure 5.1). This theme is pursued on pages 32 to 37 of *Logic and Psychology* with respect to which the translator notes: "The table of sixteen propositional operations is isomorphic with a truth-value table for two propositions, in which all the possible products are listed."

The difference, of course, is that we have linked *each* of the four connectives in the truth table columns with one specific mental process and developmental stage. Since each operation includes (nests) the less complex operations, the bi-conditional if-and-only-if (our parallel processing) does encompass all four columns with sixteen operations, just as Piaget describes for his formal operational stage. But then so does the conditional if-then (our serial process) encompass the first three columns with twelve of the sixteen operations; the conjunctive and-and (our cumulative process) encompasses the first two columns with eight of the sixteen operations; and the disjunctive or-or (our declarative process) encompasses the first column with four of the sixteen operations. If we are right in our conclusions, Piaget was looking at the four mental processes in his creative preoccupation with modern propositional logic, but did not quite notice them in the truth table columns.

The fourth similarity between the two systems takes us into the very heart of Piaget's developmental stages as compared with our recursive theory of complexity of mental processing. Thus a clear connection exists between Piaget's fourth or operational stage and our if-and-only-if parallel processing. He describes the operational stage in terms of the bringing together of multiple series, just as we do for parallel processing. Thus the operational stage has "two important acquisitions. First, the logic of propositions, which is a general structure coordinating the various logical operations (serial) into a single system. Second, a series of operational schemata which have no apparent connection with each other nor with the logic of propositions"[10] (but which the child connects). This formulation and his example are strikingly similar to our formulation of parallel processing. And as we have noted above, he also explicitly describes his fourth stage in terms of if-and-only-if operations encompassing all the sixteen truth table operations, just as we do.

An equally clear and explicit connection exists between Piaget's third concrete operational stage and our third serial if-then processing. Piaget is quite specific. In relation to the concrete operational stage he writes: "A second equally important operational system is *seriation* (italics his) or the linking of asymmetrical transitive relations into system."[11] And seriation is directly comparable to serial processing.

There is a less obvious, but nevertheless likely, similarity between Piaget's second stage, the pre-operational stage, and our second category, cumulative and-and processing. As Piaget explicitly states, his pre-operational stage is pre-serial in that "there is an absence of operational transitivity . . . the child's judgments of quantity lack systematic transitivity."[12] In our terms "pre-serial" suggests cumulative and-and processing, and this notion is supported by the examples of pre-operational problem solving, which are and-and rather than disjunctive or-or in form.

It is when we come to Piaget's formulation of his first sensory-motor stage that it would appear that there is no relationship between the two constructions. For, where Piaget provides for one single stage, our hypothesis provides for five categories of mental complexity; namely, category AV1 (concrete verbal order of information complexity, or-or disjunctive declarative processing), and four additional categories of mental complexity in the pre-verbal gestural AG order of information complexity. But then the realization sets in that there may be more similarity here than meets the eye, in Piaget's division of his first (sensory-motor) stage into six sub-stages. For what he describes as sensory-motor is pre-verbal in the same sense as our use of gestural. Consider the following:

First, Piaget's sub-stages one and two are strikingly similar to our AG1 first category of mental processing (or-or disjunctive) within our pre-verbal

---

10. *ibid.* page 22.
11. *ibid.* page 14.
12. *ibid.* page 12.

gestural order of information complexity. In the first place, the two sub-stages show little significant difference from each other, and Cole and Cole,[13] for example, treat them together as one. In these sub-stages the infant carries out single actions that are pleasurable in themselves, but with little or no understanding and action that could lead, in our terms, to cumulative and-and processing.

Second, Piaget's sub-stage three, secondary circular reactions, in which infants can now be observed to be repeating actions that give them pleasure, has very much the feel of capability for and-and processing, as for example, in pushing a hanging rattle time after time to hear the sound.

Third, Piaget's sub-stage four has the quality of our AG3 category of pre-verbal seriation—or if-then conditional serial processing. In this sub-stage the infant is described as able to combine schemas to achieve a desired effect by coordinating secondary circular reactions. The if-then quality of the behavior (that leads to Piaget's description of this sub-stage as the earliest form of problem solving) shows in this description of his ten-month-old son's successfully demonstrating the ability to realize that *if* he dropped a tin over a basin, *then* it would fall into the basin and make an interesting sound. "Now at once, Laurent takes possession of the tin, holds out his arm and drops it over the basin. I moved the latter as a check. He nevertheless succeeded several times in succession, in making the object fall in the basin."[14]

Fourth, Piaget's sub-stage five is similar to our AG4 category of mental processing—pre-verbal parallel processing in gesture. He formulates the sub-stage five, tertiary circular reactions, as focused upon the relationship between the child's body and the child's objects, thereby making the world more complex and making it possible to carry out "experiments in order to see." Thus, for example, he describes one of his children playing with a number of objects, and when one of the objects "falls in a new position, he lets it fall two or three times more in the same place, as though to study the spatial relations; then he modifies the situation."[15] Such descriptions fit readily into the idea of parallel processing in manual gesture behavior.

---

13. Cole and Cole (1993) *The Development of Children*, page 187.
14. Piaget (1952) *The Origins of Intelligence in Children*, page 255.
15. *ibid.* page 269.

What then of Piaget's sub-stage six? He himself describes it as showing the "beginnings of symbolic representation: images and words come to stand for familiar objects."[16] In other words, it corresponds to our category AV1, the first level or-or verbal processing.

In summary, our hypothesis is that Piaget's sub-stages in the sensory-motor stage would correspond as follows with our recursive hierarchy of mental processes. But, of course, Piaget allows only for one set of stages, and does not provide for recursion either above or below his major stages. We shall discuss this question of recursion in the next section.

Figure 7.4
Complexity of Mental Processes and Piaget Stages

Orders of Information Complexity	Piaget Stages	Mental Processes
Symbolic	No stages defined	B2 and-and conjunctive B1 or-or disjunctive
Verbal Concrete	Formal operational Concrete operational Pre-operational Sub-stage six	AV4 if-and-only-if parallel AV3 if-then serial AV2 and-and conjunctive AV1 or-or disjunctive
Gestural Concrete Sensory-motor Pre-verbal	Sub-stage five Sub-stage four Sub-stage three Sub-stages one and two	AG4 if-and-only-if parallel AG3 if-then serial AG2 and-and conjunctive AG1 or-or disjunctive

16. Cole and Cole (1993) *The Development of Children*, page 217.

A Recursive System

From the foregoing section, it will be apparent that a major difference between our position and Piaget's theoretical system is that we have been led by our findings into a working assumption that there exists a recursive hierarchy of orders of complexity of information, with a recurrence of the four types of mental processing within each order. That Piaget eschews such a position is clear from the fact that he chose a conception of sub-stages for analyzing his sensory-motor stage, rather than noting the possibility that we have described above, that he had in fact constructed a second set of stages.

Kurt Fischer[17] has noted this possible shortcoming in developmental theory. He has constructed a systematic hierarchy of skill levels, operating in a recurring pattern of what he calls tiers, with groupings of four skill levels within each tier: tier I, levels 1, 2, 3, 4; tier II, levels 4, 5, 6, 7; tier III, levels 7, 8, 9, 10.[18]

His use of a recursive hierarchy of groups of levels is very much in line with our own approach. However, like Piaget, his data are limited to childhood, and cover only his first two tiers (Levels 1 to 7). He comments on this problem (page 495): "Following the recurring cycle, abstractions should develop through Levels 7 to 10. . . . Because so little research has been done on cognitive development beyond adolescence, however, no data are available to provide a strong test of such predictions."[19]

Our data, of course, are about cognitive development throughout adulthood, and have been accumulating for some thirty-five years. We have found substantial evidence of a recursive process in adulthood, and have extrapolated back into childhood, overlapping in a significant way with a re-interpretation of Piaget's theory. Another attempt to go beyond

---

17. Fischer (1980) "A Theory of Cognitive Development."

18. It is interesting to note that Fischer repeats the top level of each tier, to become the bottom level of the next higher tier. In similar, but not identical vein, Jaques found it useful in relation to organizational hierarchies, to arrange our categories of mental processing into "quintaves", that is to say into groups of five, comprising, for example, categories (B1, B2, B3, B4, and C1), and then categories (C1, C2, C3, C4, D1). The category at the top of each quintave was taken as the bottom of the next higher quintave, like the note at the top of each octave in music.

19. *ibid.* page 495.

Piaget's fourth final operations stage, and into adult development, has been made by M.J. Commons, F.A. Richards, and C. Armon.[20] They have constructed three additional stages, called systematic, meta-systematic, and cross-paradigmatic reasoning. From our point of view, however, they are too heavily focused upon elements and types of problems. It is also difficult to get a tight grip on the distinctions they seek to draw between, for example, systems and fields. One of the consequences of their approach is that they encounter difficulties in quantificative scoring, not altogether resolved by choice theory as propounded by Coombs, Dawes, and Tversky. If the validity of our proposition, that there exists an objectively observable recursive pattern of four mental processes, is reinforced by further studies, then many of the above problems will be resolved. Despite these observations, however, it is interesting to note that there is growing dissatisfaction with the notion that cognitive maturation ends in adolescence.

Some Differences from Current Developmental Theory

There are thus elements of commonality between our hypotheses and Piaget and current developmental theory. There are also some significant differences. One issue in which we differ from most developmental psychologists lies in the fact that our data gathered since 1956[21] have led us to the construction of the multi-track array of maturation bands described above. Our proposition is that individuals do not mature along one and the same band, but rather along one, and one only, of a number of possible bands.

This proposition is related to a second difference; namely, that there are not just four stages, but anywhere up to fifteen or more stages (stages in Piaget's terms, categories of mental complexity in ours), produced by the recursive appearance of the four mental processes within higher and higher orders of complexity of the information processed.

Both these propositions then link with a third important difference; namely, that there is no single end point (such as the operational stage) towards which all individuals mature, but rather that each person is

---

20. Commons, Richards and Armon, Eds. (1984) *Beyond Formal Operations.*
21. See Jaques (1961) *Equitable Payment* and (1968) *Progression Handbook.*

constitutionally set to mature towards one or another of the fifteen or more categories of mental complexity, passing successively through each of the less complex categories of mental complexity on the way. We have referred to this high point as the individual's potential capability mode. It is this fact of the maturation towards different modes that produces the different maturation bands along which individuals grow. There is a discrete band for each mode, as illustrated in the figure 7.1.

Finally, it will be noted that our evidence is that individuals continue to mature throughout life, from infancy through late adulthood, in complexity of mental processing (potential capability). Even Piaget appears to have been encumbered by the unproven assumption that has dominated psychology since Binet, that intelligence, so-called, matures until about 18 years of age, and from then on, any growth in capability comes about through education and the accumulation of experience.

A Continuing Problem

A serious continuing problem at the time of writing is our failure to have constructed adequate boundary definitions and terminology for the orders of complexity of information. Simply to call them gestural pre-verbal (AG), concrete verbal (AV), verbal symbolic (B), abstract conceptual (C), and universal (D), is far from good enough.

We believe we have successfully avoided the problem in our research, because we have had to deal only with two orders of information complexity, B and C. It has been easy enough to cope with those two orders, because the contrast between them in information complexity is so great as to make it possible to handle the differences descriptively.

But this descriptive approach does not even begin to explain in systematic terms what those steps in order of complexity of information are all about. Our current direction of research is to investigate the possibility that Gibson and Isaac[22] have hit upon the true nature of these steps in their analysis of levels of abstraction in logical symbolism. Their work points to the following conceptualization of orders of information complexity as illustrated in figure 7.5.

---

22. Jaques, Gibson, Isaac (1978) *Levels of Abstraction in Logic and Human Action*, chapter 10.

The full meaning of these concepts in analyzing order of complexity of information remains to be sorted out. We believe we are on a sound track.

Figure 7.5
Orders of Information Complexity

Levels of Abstraction		Orders of Information Complexity	
V	Operation of logical domains and universe of discourse (existential and universal quantifiers).	D	Universal
IV	Classes of relationship: ordered pairs, with symmetry and transitivity.	C	Abstract conceptual
III	Classes of entities: (classification).	B	Symbolic
II	Use of words for absent concrete entities.	AV	Verbal concrete
I	Use of gestures for concrete entities at hand (pre-verbal).	AG	Pre-verbal gestural

The Mental Processes and the Number Scales

As we go to press we include a final observation, because it serves to lend further support to the conclusion that the four mental processes are fundamental features of human thought. Just as we noted the relationship between the four processes and the truth-value tables in symbolic logic, we recently noted a further connection; namely, with the four basic types of numbering used in quantitative scaling.

Nominal numbering is used where you have a population of things in no special order, and you wish to identify them. You can use numbers as names, as for example, in numbering the members of a baseball team or in zip codes. All the real numbers can be used, both positive and negative, to infinity at both ends. Such numbering is an *or-or process*, in the sense that this player could be number 6 *or* 8 *or* 22; it does not matter so long as he or she has an identification number.

Ordinal scale numbering is used where you have a population rank-ordered by judgment; as for example, in the outcome of a race, or where you have, say, a dozen objects *judged* to be of different size (but not measured). Under these conditions you can use number 1, 2, 3, 4, 5, . . . etc., to identify the order; that is to say, 1 came in first, or was largest, 2 came in second, or was the next largest, and so on; or, the building was taller than the tree, and the tree was taller than the fence. Such numbering is an *and-and process*, in the sense that Susan is 1 because she came in first, *and* Anita was 2 because she came in second, *and* so on, but you do not know by how much each came in ahead of the other—or in the case of the height of the objects, you do not note by how much each was taller than the other.

Interval scale numbering is used where you have a number of things that are not only quantitatively greater or lesser than each other, but where the size of the interval between p and q is subject to the same principle as the size of the interval between q and r, etc., because there is some operational relationship between them. Both positive and negative numbers can be used if the series is open at both ends (i.e., there is no zero starting point); as for example, the Centigrade or Fahrenheit temperature scales, or a well-ordered rating scale, say, for political conservatism. Under these conditions, you can use numbers, say, -4, -3, -2, -1, 0, +1, +2, +3, to order the ratings in series from very cold to very hot, or from very weakly conservative to very strongly so. Such numbering is an *if-then-then serial process* in the sense that *if* temperature or rating p is 23, *then* q is 24, and *if* q is 24, *then* r is 25, and so on; that is to say, if you know any two ratings, you know how much greater one is than the other (but not their ratios).

Ratio scale numbering is used where you have a number of things that are not only quantifiable in series of equal intervals, but where each of the things is measurable in absolute size, in terms of some property such as length, say, or weight, or temperature (Kelvin scale). Under such conditions it is possible to state ratios; e.g., that p is twice as long as q. Such numbering is a bi-conditional *if-and-only-if* process, in that not only is an if-then series necessary in order to get ratio comparisons, but you can get such a ratio *if-and-only-if* in addition you can measure object-size in terms of some property. Under such conditions, positive numbers only can be used (i.e., you cannot have an object that weighs -3 pounds), and zero is true zero in the sense that it means no object at all.

Our conclusion is that just as in the case of symbolic logic, Boole discovered that human thought had created the four logical connections, so in the case of the construction of number scaling systems for counting and measuring, human thought has come up with four, and only four, methods of scaling, that are generated by using the four methods of mental processing.

8

Applications and Speculations

The possibility of there being a readily accessible means for recognizing and for articulating the potential capability of each person from childhood to old age, regardless of gender, color, race, ethnic background, or even education or occupational opportunity, could have substantial and far-reaching consequences in many areas of society. We shall survey a number of these possible consequences. Some are fairly clear; others are more speculative.

Fair Employment Practices and Opportunities

It is interesting to imagine a society in which it was not possible to be mistaken about the true potential capability of any individual. Employers, educators, and other selectors, might deny what they know. They could turn the other way, but they would not be able to do so without knowing that they were doing it. And everybody else would also know it.

The evaluation of equal opportunity in managerial organizations would become a straightforward and unequivocal matter. The question would be: how many employees are involuntarily performing in roles at levels of work (measured in time-span) below their potential capability (underutilized)? Are there any identifiable categories—e.g., women, African-Americans, Hispanics, etc.—who have a significantly higher rate of underutilization than holds true generally of the more favored majority in the organization? If so, is there any explanation other than unfair employment practices at work? If you add to this analysis an equivalent survey of pay levels in relation to measured levels of work, you have a complete picture of the extent of conformity in the organization both to equal opportunity and to truly equal pay for equal level of work.

We are quite aware that this analysis is geared to equal opportunity in terms of the potential capability of people and not in terms of their applied capability in their current roles, and would indeed emphasize this morally positive outlook. For except under special circumstances (such as seeking lighter work because of heavy home duties, or pursuing higher education, or chronic illness), people yearn for work opportunities at levels consistent with their potential capability. And if they do not have the necessary skilled knowledge for work in which they are interested, and in which they could exercise their full potential, then there need to be opportunities for acquiring that skilled knowledge.[1] We need to be clear. A free-enterprise pluralist democracy that does not provide opportunity for its citizens to utilize their full *potential* capabilities in their employment work is a fundamentally evil and wasteful society. It fails to utilize its prime wealth—the potential of its people. It disaffects its people by leaving them frustrated and ill-served by boring work.

The constructive application by a nation of a means of knowing whether or not its citizens have the opportunity for work into which they can enter enthusiastically and from which they may gain a fair differential economic status lays the necessary foundation for a decent life and the sustainment of decent values and honesty based upon economic trust and justice.

Fair Employment Practices for Career and Talent Pool Development and Selection

It will be self-evident that to possess a truly objective method of evaluating not only the current potential capability of individuals, but their future potential as well, is a boon not only to effective selection for employment, but also to effective talent pool development in employment organizations. Jaques and Clement have detailed the procedures for doing so in a recent book.[2] This book was finished just as we had completed our

---

1. Jaques (1982) *Free Enterprise, Fair Employment*.
2. Jaques and Clement (1991) *Executive Leadership*, chapters 9 and 11.

analysis of results of our research. It made all the difference in the world to be able to consider managerial leadership accountability for selection, career development, and talent pool development in the light of evidence that individual potential capability could be objectively evaluated specifically in relation to the stratification of roles.

We are undertaking development work now in a few requisitely organized companies in teaching these concepts to managers as part of a more general program in which managers-once-removed are held accountable for career development of subordinates-once-removed, and for talent pool development. We have found that it is generally true that managers-once-removed can make accurate evaluations of current potential capability and the future potential over the ensuing one to five years, so long as they are making these judgments in relation to a well-established requisite organizational stratification that they understand. The possibility that such judgments could accurately be made, was of course tested in the present research, and strongly supported by the very high inter-rater reliability between the ratings of the subjects' current potential capability made by the MoRs, managers, and the subjects themselves.

The fairness of this procedure is underpinned in three ways. First, the MoR and his or her immediate subordinates must share with each other in open meeting their initial judgments of the current potential of their subordinates-once-removed. It is only after they have discussed these judgments and compared them with each other that a working conclusion is reached. Second, each one must then discuss the individual judgments with each subordinate-once-removed, as the commencement of an ongoing mentoring process. Third, the judgments are then reviewed periodically as part of the on-going mentoring and career development process. The fact that these judgments are reviewed in this way with the individuals imposes a strong discipline on the procedure.

The object of the training to be given is to assist managers-once-removed to make more self-assured evaluations of the potential of subordinates-once-removed and to be able to carry out more assured career development discussions with them, once they have an understanding of the underlying nature of mental processing and its relationship to organizational structure. *It is specifically not the intention that they be trained to listen for mental process as a "test" of potential; but rather that in getting used to the ideas, they will be able to hold them in the backs of their minds to facilitate the articulation of their gut-feel judgments.* A "test" implies right or wrong answers calculated by using criteria valued by the designer of the test. Trust-inducing working relationships between managers, managers-once-removed, subordinates, and subordinates-once-removed require that managerial judgment be used (informed by the experience of working with the individual subordinate) regarding the subordinate's current and future potential—not the use of tests designed by others that would allow a statement to be made without personal working knowledge of the individual. Our initial experience has been that simply to have these ideas in mind lets them be used as organizers, helping to focus our experience of others so that a sense of their potential capability emerges fairly quickly.

In the light of our research findings we now believe that tests, administered either by internal or external experts, should not be used for evaluating the potential capability of people already employed in the company. It is important that these evaluations should be made by MoRs, calibrated and controlled, by the gearing process described in *Executive Leadership*.[3] By this procedure an undisturbed human relationship is maintained between MoR and SoR, and sets a solid foundation for mentoring. Independent evaluations can only interfere with this delicate and important relationship—and in any case any "expert" judgments, dependent as they are upon the skill of any given expert, are likely most often to be less accurate than the MoR judgments.

This approach leads to an exceptionally fair procedure with respect to internal promotions. It makes it possible to identify everyone in the company who has the judged potential to work at the level of a vacant role, but who is currently underemployed, or who has been overpromoted. By this means *everyone* with the necessary potential, regardless of gender, color, ethnic background, age, etc., can be identified in creating a first slate for selection. Software that has been developed for this mapping will print such a list.[4]

We have also found that evaluation of level of current potential capability by evaluation of complexity of mental processing in the course

---

3. *ibid.*

4. *Requisite Organization Talent Pool Development Software,* Ver. 1.2, Cason Hall & Co. Publishers, Falls Church, VA.

of screening interviews with *external* applicants can be an important adjunct to screening for selection. It is not difficult to train such interviewers. And the procedure is ethical because external applicants know they are in a selection assessment situation.

It is our view that as these ideas become more widely known and familiar, they will lead to people's becoming familiar with their own and others' potential capability as a matter of ordinary everyday interaction. And that will be that. Nothing unusual; nothing extraordinary; just an ordinary part of our knowledge about each other. And the ultimately crucial point is this—it will be accurate knowledge, in contrast to the judgments we always have made anyhow, whose degree of accuracy we could never know since we never had an effective way of articulating them. *And the procedures that follow from these ideas have the distinction of contributing positively to fair employment practices.*

A Matter of Organizational Theory

Our findings give, at long last, a theoretical explanation of why the managerial hierarchy has existed for 3,000 years, why it is so ubiquitous today, and why, despite the unsupported predictions of so many organizational gurus, it is unlikely ever to go away.

Our argument is that it takes someone who is capable of working at one stratum higher than immediate subordinates to be an effective managerial leader of those subordinates: at Stratum II to manage Stratum I, up to Stratum VII to manage Stratum VI. If we simply translate that finding into mental processing, it would take someone at the next higher category of complexity of mental process to have the potential capability to be a successful managerial leader of immediate subordinates at the next lower category of complexity of mental process and of potential capability. That is to say, it would require a cumulative processor to give effective managerial leadership to a declarative processor, a serial processor to a cumulative processor, a parallel processor to a serial processor, a third order declarative processor to a second order parallel processor, and so on up the scale.

But why should this one step up in mental capability be necessary for effective managerial work? There is a face validity answer in the conception of managerial leadership described in Jaques and Clement's book *Executive Leadership*,[5] namely, that the essence of effective discharge of their leadership accountabilities by managers is that they shall in the first place be capable of setting the wider directional context within which those subordinates can carry out their work. Managerial leadership depends upon other managerial practices as well, but nothing can be done unless an adequate directional context is set. For it is this context that provides the setting in which subordinates can get on with their own work, and in collaboration with each other, using their judgment and making decisions secure in the knowledge of the overarching context that has been set for them.

The idea of an adequate context is a psychologically interesting one. It is a context that is "just right"—neither "too narrow" nor yet "too broad." For if it is too narrow, subordinates will feel too constrained, too restricted, too tightly reined in, frustrated by a micro-manager experienced as breathing down their necks. And if it is too broad, they will feel unorganized, lost, directionless, flapping in the wind, worried by a manager who is too distant, who leaves them unclear about where exactly they are all going, and who expects them to understand too much.

Our hypothesis is that the optimum conditions are precisely those that are provided by one-step differences in mental processing between effective managerial leaders and their immediate subordinates. Cumulative processors can set just the right context for declarative processors because it is in their ability to make the connections that can bind together separate unconnected pieces of information. Serial processors can set context for cumulative processors by providing the chains of causal consequences within which their subordinates' cumulatively organized judgments and decisions are planned to flow. Parallel processors can set context for serial processors because they can provide the connecting framework between the multiple series each of which their subordinates are pursuing, a framework that gives just the right immediate setting in the way that a PERT chart based upon a critical path analysis provides the context for the various pathways involved in a multi-project program. Third order declarative processors can provide context for second order parallel processors because the higher order complexity of the information they use can encompass and pull together the consequential cause-and-effect processing

5. Jaques and Clement (1991) *Executive Leadership*.

at the lower order of information complexity in the way that abstract concepts can be used to pull together and organize large amounts of everyday verbal symbolic information. And then the context setting repeats itself (a recursive process) as you move to the third order complexity cumulative, serial and parallel processing of Stratum VI, VII, and VIII.

There is a possible general picture here of a hierarchy of levels of complexity within which the human mind organizes, stores, and processes information, with clusters of more detailed and less complex information nested within larger and more complex interacting clusters, with active interchange and interplay going on continuously between clusters at various levels. The higher the level of complexity of mental processing a given individual has the current potential to exercise, then the larger and more complex are the information fields that can be handled and the more complex the problems that can be successfully tackled—always dependent, of course, upon the individual's valuing the work, for that determines the mental energy that will be brought to bear upon the processing work, and upon the individual's possessing the necessary skilled knowledge, for that determines whether the individual has sufficient available stored information to be manipulated automatically (i.e., in a skilled manner).[6]

Finally, our formulation also gives a possible explanation of another general finding about the managerial hierarchy. That finding is that in larger corporations, that is to say, corporations whose top CEO role is at Stratum VI (time-span 10 to 20 years), or at Stratum VII (20 to 50 years), or at Stratum VIII (50 years—or three generations—plus), it is optimum to organize by placing true profit-and-loss account, market oriented, strategic business units at Stratum V. This arrangement leaves the true corporate strategic levels at Stratum VI, with business unit presidents in Stratum V roles managing subordinates at Stratum IV and below in running a coherent integrated business, and interacting with Stratum VI and above in influencing corporate strategy to provide the broad business context and policies necessary for the successful operation of the business unit in its market.

Now, let it be noted, first, that a Stratum V business unit president's role calls for third order declarative processing. That provides, on the one

---

6. See the discussion of mental processing, values, and skilled knowledge, in Jaques and Clement (1991) *Executive Leadership*, chapter 2.

hand, for effective context setting and managerial leadership for a subordinate organization, all of which is at second order complexity of information dealing with the marketplace in terms of the everyday order of verbal symbolic information, and on the other hand, it provides for a president able to interact within the third order level of information complexity with corporate executives, all of whom ought to be working with such information.

Let it be noted, second, that it provides for a group of corporate executives operating with the abstract conceptual order of information complexity needed for making the international, financial, technological, human resourcing, legal, political and corporate thrusts, analyses, policies, and development work that should be the focus of work of any leading global corporation.

And so we get to the interaction between two main different types of business work: business unit profit-and-loss market work carried out in the huge population of the world of second order complexity information, led from Stratum V; and corporate strategic business work (Stratum VI, VII, and VIII) carried out in the world of third order complexity information connected with the second order world through the crucial Stratum V linchpin role which exercises leadership downwards and creates strategic links upwards.

Some Political Implications

There is one serious and far-reaching implication of our findings for political life that needs to be pointed out. With the publication of this book it becomes possible for there to be public identification of the level of potential capability of our presidents, vice presidents, prime ministers, senators, congressmen, members of parliament, heads of foreign governments, governors, state representatives, mayors, city councilors, and also key appointees, such as cabinet members, federal government political appointees, heads of agencies, and military leaders, through to such important local community figures as school superintendents, principals, and police chiefs. In addition, the heads of our great commercial, industrial, educational, and religious institutions are subject to the same scrutiny and evaluations as are the heads of departments to their own subordinates.

The reason for the transparency of potential capability of public figures is not only that they are public, but also that they are often publicly engaged in engrossed argument and debate and their mental processing is there for all to see. It is not that they are engaged in public debate all the time. Prepared speeches, for example, do not count as engrossed discussion. But television, for example, provides many opportunities for watching public figures being put under the microscope in unrehearsed interviews, and especially in televised clashes that can occur during political campaigns, or over what to do about major controversial issues such as abortion, euthanasia, drugs, crime, education, morals, and values.

During the past year the authors have tested their ability to make such judgments from television and radio broadcasts. In addition to viewing and listening, we have videotaped and audiotaped such material for subsequent scrutiny. The consistency of our independent judgments of type of mental processing has been nearly 100 percent—and in each case we can point precisely to the material that has led to our evaluations. That consistency, of course, gives evidence only of reliability, and does not provide evidence of validity of the evaluations in relation to political competence or competence in public affairs. But the match was very high between the opinions of others based upon significant supporting information about the maximum likely potential capability of those of the figures whom we had observed and the mental processing we evaluated during the television and radio broadcasts.

Picture then a world in which the current and future potential of candidates taking part in an election campaign is known to the electorate. Will it be a good thing or a bad thing? Our argument would be that on balance it is in the public interest for such evaluations to be available in articulated form. For we are trying to make these judgments anyhow. They appear in the oft asked question, "Is so-and-so big enough for president, or governor, or whatever?" or "Which of the candidates is the bigger person?" Since such questions not only do arise but indeed should arise, it is far better that they should be answered accurately. Those who seek and accept the responsibilities, the authority, and the fruits of public service should be subject to the deepest possible scrutiny of their potential capability as well as of their values and skilled knowledge, by the public who entrust them with office.

Jaques & Cason

This personal evaluation of public figures then raises an equally important related issue; namely, what is the level of work required in public offices, and therefore, what is the minimum level of potential capability that incumbents should have? This issue can be readily resolved for appointed offices, for these offices are part of the bureaucratic system. There is no difficulty, for example, in sorting out a requisite organization for civil service or social service departments in relation to the work to be done, and determining the level of work in the established roles by time-span measurement. But the issue is more difficult in the case of elected representative roles. For they are freestanding roles, and not part of the bureaucratic (managerial) hierarchy. What we would envision happening, however, is the gradual establishing of minimum levels for various representative roles, expressed in terms of the minimum levels of potential capability that should be required of candidates for election to such positions.

Thus, for example, is C3 level of potential capability—the same as a Stratum VII corporate CEO—too much to require as an absolute minimum for a U.S. president? Surely at a minimum the role calls for the ability to handle the abstract conceptual ideas and information of third order complexity, in a thoughtful manner with serial strategic thrust? National and international politics are at least this complex. This notion is reinforced by considering the issue from the point of view of time-span. Just because the presidential term of office is four years does not mean that a president should initiate only those projects that can be completed during his or her incumbency. For that would mean starting with four-year projects in the first year and reducing to one-year projects during the last year. No! Presidents of vision must initiate major developments certainly at the ten-year plus level, and we would argue that for an economic power at the scale of the United States, that level must be twenty-years plus; otherwise there would be no Tennessee Valley Authority, no man on the moon, no major defense systems, no national resource support systems, no effective immigration programs, no sustained international alliances, no adequate criminal control programs. Succeeding governments may alter these programs, but the health of the nation socially, politically, and economically will depend upon the extent to which it gets a succession of presidents of the necessary levels of potential capability to initiate or continue programs of this scale.

In a similar vein, where should we place the minimum standards of potential capability for governors, for senators, and so on down the line? We believe that it would be a boon to the political life of our society if minimum standards were publicly discussed and debated. But more than that, we have established concepts and a language by means of which they can be debated, and out of the spread of learning of the language and use of the ideas, appropriate standards will come into being.

Relevance to Education

There are many ways in which the ability to evaluate accurately the potential capability of individuals could be of benefit to our educational system. In the first place it would help to ensure that people of the necessary level of capability were being appointed to lead our schools, a condition that is far from guaranteed at present. The level of work required in school superintendent or school principal roles can accurately be measured by time-span. There is some evidence to show that they are requisitely Stratum V and Stratum IV roles respectively. It would make an enormous difference to have individuals of the necessary level of capability to fill those roles; or imagine the progress that could be achieved with so-called difficult schools if an educator with, say C1 current potential capability to work at Stratum V, were appointed into a Stratum IV school principal role—the school could well take off because of the principal's excess of capability in a way that has been observed to happen when an "outstanding" principal has taken over a "problem" school under such circumstances.

In the same vein, is it not self-evident that teaching roles should be minimally at Stratum II, and that teachers must be capable of cumulative 'and-and' processing. At any lower level, say at Stratum I with B1 mental complexity, we would have teachers capable only of rote teaching. Too many teachers are at this level, and it will not do; to be teachers' aides yes, but to be fully accountable classroom teachers, most certainly no.

With respect to the educational process itself we shall make only a brief comment because our hypotheses about the maturation of potential capability in childhood (as manifested in increasing complexity of mental process) have not as yet been validated. But many fundamental educational questions would appear quite different were it possible to separate the evaluation of potential capability from knowledge and values, and to treat the acquisition and regurgitation of knowledge and the influencing of values separately from the recognition that potential capability will mature regardless of the educational process and of the degree to which pupils value and are committed to that process.

Thus, for example, if potential capability matures, is there any reason to have pass-fail criteria determining whether pupils move from one grade to the next, rather than enabling pupils to progress in accord with their maturing potential and encouraging the accumulation of such skilled knowledge as might be possible with that potential? Or are there circumstances in which pupils should be grouped, perhaps for special purposes, or on special occasions, in terms of their potential capability rather than in terms of their ability to ingest masses of information and to earn high marks on examinations?

This distinction between the earning of high marks (or even IQ levels) and current potential capability (now that it is likely to be measurable) goes to the heart of the meaning of education.[7] It raises questions, for example, about the criteria we use for admission to our universities. There is little reason to believe that SAT scores, any more than IQ, are uniquely related to potential capability. Should there not be some weighing of potential capability along with examination results in our allocation of university places, especially where resources are in short supply? SAT scores are of some use in indicating how students have used their potential capability. But they are far from the whole story of the level of employment work that graduates will have the potential eventually to achieve.

It is not our intention to try to answer questions such as these at this stage. We do intend, however, to show that the whole current approach to educational philosophy, theory, and practice would have to undergo a substantial re-think were this view accepted—that the educational process can affect the acquisition of knowledge and of the socialization of values, but that the maturation of potential capability goes on under its own steam, that its level and progress are measurable, and that its level of maturation at any point in adulthood will be the main determinant of the level of work that each individual will have the potential to carry at that point.

---

7. See Jaques (1970) "Learning for Uncertainty", reprinted (1990) *Creativity and Work.*

The acquisition of skilled knowledge is important. The development of requisite social values is critical. But they do not influence the potential capability of individuals, and it is the reliable provision of the opportunity for everyone to use that potential that is the hallmark of the good democratic free enterprise society. Our educational system must have, as one of its central pillars, the ability to recognize the maturing potential capability of each of its students, and the provision of the opportunity for them to experience the full use of that potential in their studies.

Artistic Creativity and Capability

What makes for greatness in artistic creativity, like leadership, has always had a mystical magical quality. These qualities tend to be explained in terms of special personality qualities, and with unconscious processes based on the resolved and unsolved experiences and conflicts of infancy and childhood. There are long lists of special personality qualities such as pro-active originality, imaginativeness, self-control, tenacity, and sometimes anxiety, emotional instability or even insanity, that are considered assets for "truly" creative work.

Apart from the last three items (the -T items), all of these qualities are part of the ordinary makeup of ordinary people engaged in the business of everyday work and play for survival, adaptation, and growth. They are concerned with any and every kind of work, and so long as they are not present in the form of work-inhibiting psychopathology (-T), none of them plays any special or specific part in creativity and work. What is necessary for work of particular kinds are the variables we have set out in our analysis; namely, complexity of mental processing (CMP), valuing (V) of the work, and having the necessary skilled knowledge (K/S) to be able to do it. These variables are the same as those which can explain the quality of greatness in so-called creative work. Indeed, our unequivocal view is that all work is creative, and to talk about creative ability as something special and different from working ability is simply wrong: they are the same thing. All work is creative.

There is one seeming exception to the above view of the identical nature of creativity and work; namely, so-called artistic creativity—or artistic work. It is, however, only a seeming exception. For artistic work is work like any other work, in the sense of using judgment in making decisions in order to accomplish an output, or opus. And just as for any work, the creation of a work of art requires that the artist intensely values (V) producing such work, has developed the necessary skilled knowledge (K/S) to have the technique for doing so, and is free from such psychopathology (-T) as would interfere with or inhibit the working (whatever other effects on the artist's life and behavior, such as, for example, cutting off an ear, any such psychopathology might have).

What is special about artistic work is that it is the production of one person, from beginning to end, and it comes from inside that person. That person gets the idea and carries it out to completion, himself or herself (although assistants may at times be employed to carry out the intentions of an artist, under detailed instruction and supervision). The opus has to do with the external representation of one person's internal state of mind. To the extent that the opus is based upon explicit copying of nature, it becomes less of a work of art.

An important consequence of this totally personal quality of the production of a work of art is that it is possible to observe in the work itself evidence of the complexity of mental process of the artist him or herself. Our current hypothesis is that it is this level of complexity that is uniquely and directly related to our experience of the greatness of a work of art. In short, given different artists working with full commitment and full use of skilled knowledge, what makes for our experience of a greater or lesser work of art is our direct sense of the level of complexity of mental process with which the work has been woven together and which shows in the observable complexity of structure of the work itself.

These differences in complexity are visible in paintings, for example, in the nature of the movement on the canvas. In the category B, second order complexity (everyday symbolic) paintings, the eye can move where it will; you can fix readily upon any object or detail without being moved away; and your eye can move out to the frame, and cross it, without any sense of being pulled back into the picture. Such paintings are the work of the Sunday painters, or mass production artists.

In the category C, third order complexity (abstract conceptual), we move into the levels of what become accepted as great art. Here mental complexity shows in a quite different way. The picture is on the move. The eye literally gets pulled about within the picture, and it requires effort to stop and examine details. There is movement out towards the frame, but on approaching the frame the eye gets pulled back into the picture and on its way again. Even in still life paintings, the eye cannot remain still as it observes the objects—outlines which appear to be clearcut in fact turn out to be much less so. This quality of movement is known to many art scholars and specialists.[8]

Then there are paintings—very few—with a much more complex pattern of movement, which we hypothesize are the expressions of category D, fourth order level of complexity of mental processing. Here the eye is pulled not only round the picture, but there is a further pulsating movement into and out of the picture from front to back, so that the figures or objects appear to be moving in three-dimensional space, as in the effect obtained with three-dimensional pictures seen with special colored spectacles. The experience is a riot of movement as in the Sistine Chapel.

In addition to these broad categories of complexity of paintings which we are relating to orders of complexity of information, there are visible complexities of relationships within each order, that closely resemble the four patterns of complexity of mental processing. In brief: there are pictures with a number of unrelated focal points—declarative; pictures with one simple focal point or action—cumulative; pictures which are organized with apparent actions or movement from one focal point towards another—serial; and pictures with complex patterns of interaction between sets of related focal points—parallel.

It is not, however, our intention in this brief account of hypotheses about the nature of perceived greatness in art, to prove or disprove or to elaborate these hypotheses. We have, rather, two other things in mind.

First, we wish to give an indication of just how extensive the implications of our findings about complexity of mental processing may turn out to be. We are currently, for example, looking for equivalent signs of complexity in music and in poetry, and expect to find them. The point is that these patterns of mental process suffuse all human work activity. They are ubiquitous and are to be observed under all circumstances wherever there are active human beings—be they infants, children, or young, middle-aged or older adults.

---

8. See, for example, Viktor Zuckerkandl's description in his work *Sound and Symbol.*

Second, if our analysis of works of art is correct, it demonstrates just how sensitive we are to expression and complexity of mental processing in ourselves and others. What we think of as greatness in human beings is likely to be a function more of our sensing of their manifesting high levels of mental complexity, than of the use, for example, of color or visual conflict by artists, or the possession of outstanding personality characteristics by our political leaders.

The Utilization of a Nation's Talent

The idea that the greatest resource of a nation (or of any social institution) is its human talent, is an old and well-worn cliché. What is less of a cliché and more of a social headache is the fact that nowhere is there any guarantee that this self-evident idea will be systematically applied. For there are two great obstacles standing in the way of its use. The first obstacle consists of the myriad social arrangements such as class and caste structures, the role of women, the position of minorities, the uneven access to education, that can militate against talent coming into its own. The second obstacle consists of the serious shortcomings everywhere that mar the procedures that do exist for bringing the necessary levels of talent into play.

One major expression of the problem is the difficulty in America, for example, in ensuring continuity in high level talent at the top of the large corporations. Great industrial leaders like Alfred P. Sloan, founder of General Motors, and Thomas Watson, who founded IBM, may build up these corporations. But there are no guarantees that their successors will have the levels of capability to sustain the businesses, let alone develop them further.

When the successors have lesser capability, they inevitably pull the institutions down to their own level as has been the case for all to see in the vicissitudes of companies like General Motors and IBM. Indeed, the frequency of the downswings brought about by successors at lower levels of capability has given rise to the theory propounded by academics, of the natural life cycle of companies—a cycle of growth in the early and middle years followed by old age decline. This theory may sound good, but it is false. For whether or not a company declines at any stage will be largely determined by the level of capability of its senior executives, and not by some natural law of companies.

Where the level of capability of its executives is sustained, companies can and will continue to prosper—Mitsui has done so for over three hundred years. The trouble is that there are flaws in the succession procedures. For example, there is a widespread tendency for boards of directors to abdicate their duty to find and choose a new chief executive: they leave it to the retiring chief executive and the old boy network. This flaw is exacerbated when the chief executive is also the board chairman. The trouble is that it is difficult for involved executives to find and choose individuals as big as themselves, or indeed, bigger.

Then there are the incorrect assumptions about capability in old age. The western world not only tends not to revere its oldest citizens, but also fails to recognize that its highest level talent continues to mature at a rapid rate throughout the later years—unless premature senile physiological deterioration sets in. Thus for a nation to retire top executives at the age of sixty-five, or even at sixty-two or sixty as the fashion dictates, is plumb social craziness. It takes, for example, the mode C4 individuals and retires them when they are working at C3 (Stratum VII), and throws away the use of their C4 talent that will mature and become available when they are between sixty-five and seventy-five years of age. The best Japanese companies do not, of course, do anything so wasteful. Many of their most senior executives are employed effectively well into their seventies.

This waste of talent at the top is mirrored in an equivalent waste at the lower layers. There is a widespread tendency to underemploy large sectors of the population with level B2 current potential capability (CPC) in Stratum I roles in large-scale offices and stores and mass production factories. This underemployment is a major source of industrial stress and unrest.

Full Employment of Potential and the Good Society

But what should the community do? There are many answers to this question, many things that must be done. But there is one condition that must be achieved that is absolutely fundamental. It underlies all others. Without it we shall never have the good democratic society which people of good will everywhere so ardently seek. Failure to achieve it so far is the Achilles heel of our approach towards that good society. The absolute need for that condition flows unequivocally from our argument in this text.

The simplest statement of this basic condition is that of achieving *fair employment* throughout the nation, for everyone and forever. By fair employment we mean the following:

Fair employment is a socio-economic condition in which all people who wish to work for a living shall have a reasonable opportunity to obtain employment in a position in which they can utilize their potential capability to the fullest and for which they shall receive equitable differential compensation related to differentials in levels of work complexity.

The central point is this: the widespread and continued existence of high levels of chronic unemployment of any group in society, combined with opportunity for work only at levels substantially below potential capability even when work is available, is among the most inhuman and cancerous of all social conditions. It produces resentment and rage, social disaffection, mistrust, anxious desperation, and deep, deep, cloying depressed despair. And that is true for young people, the elderly, women, Hispanics, African-Americans, Arabs, Jews, Native Americans, and indeed for everyone in times of general economic depression.

There is nothing new about this statement. Everyone knows it. No one need be surprised by it. What is new, however, is the demonstration that every individual really does have his or her actual and measurable level of potential capability that demands an actual and measurable level of work to satisfy it, in just as real and substantial a sense as the fact that a hungry stomach requires food or the person will starve.

And for the last time in this book, we repeat: we are talking about *potential* capability both current and future. It is each person's *potential* that must be satisfied now, and with maturation, into the future. And if his or her applied capability is below potential because of lack of skilled knowledge and experience, then that lack must be made up. Fortunately, it is not too difficult to do so by special educational and crash training programs—so long as the individuals who take part have the encouraging reassurance of employment at levels of work congruent with one's potential capability.

Moreover, each person's potential capability will have matured regardless of lack of schooling, and regardless of unemployment or of ghetto conditions of life, both of which stir the full use of potential for simple survival; and it will continue to mature, and demand increasing levels of work as it does so, throughout adult life.

Jaques & Cason

The demands of individual potential capability must be met. But modern democratic societies are employment societies; that is to say, societies in which of those who work for a living, the vast majority work for a wage or salary in employment organizations. Given the moral and political will, expressed in requisite political associations that govern equally requisite behavior, the means exist for sustained consistent full employment.[9] It is our hope that as knowledge spreads about level of potential capability and how to identify it in each and every individual, it will become increasingly difficult to turn away from and deny the devastating impact on human beings and on society of failure to employ our human talent resource to the fullest. We are economically poorer for our failure to do so. And our disadvantaged minorities are not only poorer economically, they are devastatingly starved as human beings for not being able to employ their potential in socially constructive ways.

On the other hand, there is nothing more calculated to arouse satisfaction, constructive cooperation, and a sense of social justice, and to stir everyone's fulsome expression in our employment society, than the opportunity for continual use of one's potential capability in constructive work, and for fair and just differential recognition for that work. Given such conditions, the good society really is possible.

---

9. See, for example, Jaques (1982) *Free Enterprise, Fair Employment.*

Appendix A

Illustrative Case Material

In this section we give selected examples of the four types of mental processing, at the second and third orders of information complexity. It is these levels with which our research was concerned, in line with our assumptions that these were the types of mental processing that would turn out to be related to the basic layering of the managerial hierarchical employment organizations with which we were working.

Our aim in including this material is to illustrate the processes as clearly as possible, so that the reader can know the kinds of process to which we have been referring. Each of the transcripts has been annotated to point out the different processes and to help the reader identify their form. The materials have been edited only to preserve anonymity.

We have not tried to present training materials. Our experience in training has been that it requires students to have the opportunity to review many dozens of examples, in discussion with a competent tutor.

The opportunity to hear what these processes sound like is provided by an audiocassette that has been recorded by actors using transcripts of actual interviews.[1]

In annotating the illustrations, we have used both systems of terminology for categorizing mental processes: our initial system in terms of declarative, cumulative, serial, and parallel; and our recent re-conceptualization in terms of or-or disjunctive, and-and conjunctive, if-then

---

1. *Complexity of Mental Processing: How to Listen for the Four Processes.* (Falls Church, VA: Cason Hall & Co. Publishers, 1992), audiocassette, approximately 30 minutes.

conditional, and if-and-only-if bi-conditional, processing. The following descriptions of the four mental processes from chapter 2 are reprinted for your convenience while reading the interviews.

- **Declarative processing**: a person explains his or her position by bringing forward a number of separate reasons for it. The reasons are separate in the sense that each is brought forward individually, on its own, and no connection is made with any of the other reasons; for example, "Here's one reason for my idea, here's another, I could give you others as well." This method of processing has a disjunctive, declarative quality.

- **Cumulative processing**: a person explains his or her position by bringing together a number of different ideas, none of which is sufficient to make the case, but taken together, they do; for example, a detective might argue, "If you take this first point (clue), and put it together with these three other items we have observed, then it becomes clear that such-and-such has occurred." This method of processing has a pulled-together, conjunctive quality.

- **Serial processing**: a person explains his or her position by constructing a line of thought made up of a sequence of reasons, each one of which leads on to the next; thus creating a chain of linked reasons; for example, "I would do A because it would lead to B, and B will lead on to C, and C would lead on to where we want to get." This method of processing has a conditional quality in the sense that each reason in the series sets the conditions that lead to the next reason, and so on to the conclusion.

- **Parallel processing**: a person explains his or her position by examining a number of other possible positions as well, each arrived at by means of serial processing (see above). The several lines of thought are held in parallel and can be linked to each other. To take one example, it becomes possible to take useful points from less favored positions to bolster up a favored one. "If I start with a possible position that would lead to A and A to B, that would end in outcome 1, which I do not support. Or I could start with another position that would lead on to C and then to D and get to outcome 2, which

I also do not support. I like a third position because it could lead to E and then to F, and that could lead to outcome 3 that I do favor, but only if you took action B from the first series, and inserted it between steps E and F on the way to outcome 3." This method of processing has a double conditional quality, in the sense that the various scenarios are not only linked with each other, but they can condition each other as well.

In trying to identify the various types of processing, keep the following information and questions in mind:

First, attend to the pattern of development of the argument—do not get ensnared in the content and whether it is a good argument or not—and observe whether the pattern is serial or non-serial. The serial pattern is probably easiest to recognize—it is an argument in the form of A happened, and that led to B, and that led on to C, and because of C, D happened, and that in turn caused E, or in other words, if A then B, B then C, C then D, etc.

Second, if the pattern is non-serial, ask if it is simply declarative in the sense of disjunctive unrelated or-or arguments. Or, are the arguments accumulated and explicitly related to each other as a collection of important data points or reasons for the conclusion, in the form of A and B and C together. If the former, it is declarative, disjunctive or-or processing; if the latter, it is cumulative, conjunctive, and-and processing.

Third, if the pattern is serial, ask if it is composed of one or more unconnected if-then-then series without a weaving back and forth between them; or if it is composed of a number of such series connected with each other, with references back and forth between them. The unconnected if-then-then series will be in the form of if A then B, if B then C, etc. The connected multiple series will be in the form of if-and-only-if P then Q then R. If the former, it is serial conditional processing; if the latter, it is bi-conditional parallel processing.

Fourth, decide whether the individual is using second order or third order information complexity. (Refer to full discussion of the orders of information complexity on pages 32–34.)

Fifth, once you have read an interview, re-read it straight through, without pausing to read the comments. It will give a better feel of the mental processing patterns.

Subject A
B1 Declarative Or-Or Processing
Second Order Information Complexity

Interviewer: Which question do you want to start on? Legalization of drugs?

Subject A: Legalization of drugs. I would say no. There are too many out there in this country now. I think this is really going to be our downfall if they don't do something about it. *(A number of discrete articulated reasons linked to the conclusion but not verbally connected to each other. "Too many" is a good reason or "it will be our downfall" is a good enough reason.)*

Interviewer: What about the argument that if you don't legalize, it's going to get worse, because you've got all the robber barons who are making big money out of it.

Subject A: That's true, but I don't think it should be legalized. It would just be even more rampant than it is now. *(Another discrete unconnected, or-or reason.)*

Interviewer: You think there would be more drug-taking?

Subject A: Yes. There'd be more addiction. *(Another discrete unconnected or-or reason.)*

Interviewer: Anything else?

Subject A: Well, I think having more drugs around would make more crime. It would cost more and more money. *(None of the above reasons have been pulled together into an accumulated set of reasons for the conclusion. They have all been in the form of or-or statements. However, the "and" linking the last two reasons causes the interviewer to try to get the subject to expand by pushing to see if there is a more complex mental process available.)*

Interviewer: Yes? . . .

Subject A: I'm not a very good one for arguing. *(At this point the interviewer changes the topic for discussion. The method of processing in this interview is declarative processing.)*

Subject B
B2 Cumulative And-And Processing
Second Order Information Complexity

B2 Cumulative and-and processing tends to sound like a more reasoned and thoughtful discourse. The display of B2 mental processing is more likely to cause the listener to be persuaded of a point of view for the simple reason that supportive information has been articulated as an accumulated set of connected reasons for the conclusion or position.

Subject B: I'd like to talk about my job. What I see is the guys they just take advantage, you give them one little thing and they want more, want more, and want more. *(Conclusion is "the guys take advantage." Support for this conclusion is presented in two connected reasons, 1) you give them something and 2) they just want more and more.)*

Interviewer: What position are you in at the moment?

Subject B: I'm really wearing three hats at the moment. Our foreman's on holiday so I'm standing in for him as factory supervisor. Our coordinator, he's away on a course and I'm also doing his job. And, by the same token, I'm supposed to be shop steward when I'm on the floor. So really . . . *(Subject B makes the statement, "I'm really wearing three hats at the moment" and then proceeds to describe why he thinks he is wearing these hats—i.e., using cumulative and-and processing to gather a set of reasons that are articulated together to support his statement.)*

Interviewer: These three hats don't sit on your head at the same time?

Subject B: No, it's impossible. But when I'm on the floor I'm one of the guys, and then when I go in the office I see just what one of those guys are doing and I think it's really unfair. I'd probably do it myself to a point but not the whole way. They just seem to take advantage if a person's not there and they'll do more or less—virtually nothing so to speak. *(A large, articulated, accumulated and-and set of reasons in continued support of an earlier conclusion "the guys take advantage".)*

Interviewer: Who takes advantage of you?

Subject B: The guys on the floor. Whenever the foreman's not there, because I'm there or even if I'm not there, if there's ten minutes for a smoke they'll take 15 or 20 minutes. If you ask them to do something that's out of the norm, they really don't want to because it's out of their way. *(Subject B is continuing to support the earlier conclusion that "the guys take advantage." The and-and set of reasons is expressed as, 'because of A, and because of B, and because of C . . . .')*

Interviewer: They don't readily pitch in with you, that sort of thing?

Subject B: To a degree, I have a good understanding. I have a better understanding with them than the actual coordinator has.

Interviewer: What's the coordinator?

Subject B: Well, I suppose you could say the junior foreman. He's the go-between between us and the foreman. He's created a lot of problems there. It's quite a tennis match. It's back and to, it really is hard to explain, but he's created this set of rules before he was foreman. Now he finds it hard to control guys because he set the rules before he got in this position. To try and step into this position it's near an impossibility, because you're only there for one or two weeks at a time, then you're back on the floor, so you can't do anything to change anything. It's very, very hard to discipline anybody because you've got to go back out there in two weeks' time and work with that same guy. He will do a lot of shouting about people behind their backs and expecting you to tell tales on them to get the message through; well, it doesn't happen that way. And that puts the whole thing into a really difficult situation down there. *(The last arguments are showing early signs of a sequential chained relationship but are not yet linked explicitly. Subject B is using a high level of cumulative processing and will likely mature within a few years to using serial processing.)*

Re-read Subject B's interview to get the feel of the collecting of a set of and-and reasons to support a conclusion.

In the following two annotations we will use the chain, link, and relink concepts to describe the serial processing used by each subject.

Subject C
B3 Serial If-Then-Then Processing
Second Order Information Complexity

It is noteworthy in the following case that positions are supported by a build-up of reasons that Subject C relates to one another in a sequence, creating extended chains of one thing leading to another.

Subject C: Well, I'm not sure if you're aware that since the change of government which occurred in the state about eighteen months ago *(This statement of history is a clue to the listener to look for serial processing in the form of a chain of related historical events.)* a conservative government came to power in the state, *(Event A)* and they've been pushing very much to use a rules of payment principle *(A leads to B)*, and that's reaching into education. *(B leads to C. Chain #1, historical sequential relationships of A led to B, B led to C.)*

It seemed that there are a lot of areas in education that could be tightened up, particularly on teachers' conditions *(New position, link A, beginning of chain #2.)*, teachers who are retiring or taking leave *(Link B, creating A linked to B)* and coming back as casuals making a lot more money *(Link C, creating B linked to C)* and doing a lot less work, have fewer responsibilities. *(C linked to D)* This is seen as a big issue. *(D linked to E)* So this has generally led to a tightening of teachers' conditions *(E linked to F)* and that has affected the numbers of pupils in a class, which has gone up *(F linked to G)*, and that generally has caused a lot of unrest amongst teachers *(G linked to H)* and that in turn has had an effect right down through the school to the pupils. *(H linked to I) (A chain of sequential relationships regarding the consequences of use of "new rules of payment" principle in areas of education that could be tightened up.)*

I have three kids at school; one's just started high school and one has just started kindergarten. So I'm concerned how it reverberates back on children, particularly my own *(This is beginning of a new chain #3.)*; and I feel that although I don't have a lot of disagreement that certain facets of the education system needed tightening *(Link A)*, I do believe that they've gone too far and created unrest. *(A linked to B)* A lot of schools have restricted the choice of subjects available *(B linked to C)*, they've basically reduced the number of teachers available in schools *(C linked to D)* and they've increased class sizes. *(D linked to E) (A chain of five sequential relationships regarding the effect of use of "new rules of payment" on subject's school-age children.)*

Note: none of these serial arguments are relinked or rechained. They are discrete chains, therefore Subject C manifests serial processing.

Re-read Subject C's interview without the comments to note more clearly the sequential or serial pattern.

Subject D
B4 Parallel If-and-Only-If Processing
Second Order Information Complexity

Serial processes are here used in parallel, with relinking between the serial chains to create a line of reasoning in support of the subject's position on the issue, and with one conditional upon another (if-and-only-if).

Interviewer: What do you think about the legalization of drugs?

Subject D: I guess I'll start off with some overall comments. *(A person using parallel processing may start off by making a beginning overall statement of their position and then go on to explain why they hold this position by creating multiple chains of serially related reasons for not holding other positions.)* And that is that when it comes to recreational substances of any sort, I believe that history *(Look for a chained historical account.)* has shown that inordinately large amounts of money and resources can be plowed in forever to containing the proliferation of the use of those recreational substances *(Link A)* and it hardly ever works. *(A linked to B)* So that's an overall point of view. *(End of Chain #1 regarding history.)*

I would have a lot of questions about the amount of money society spends in drug control, let's just call it drugs for the minute. The second point is this *(Look for second chain.)* I think there is probably a lot of disinformation about the effects that drugs have on the human body. *(New chain, chain #2, link A.)* Let's get specific and maybe talk about heroin-injectable-type things. *(A linked to B)* Heroin as I read it—and by the way I don't even smoke and I don't drink very much and I'm not personally a user of these things—but, as I read it, understand it, pure heroin is not particularly addictive *(B linked to C)*, it's not particularly detrimental to the human body *(C linked to D)*, it's all the things that come with the illicit use of these products that cause the damage. *(D linked to E, end of chain #2 regarding effect on the body of illegal heroin-type drugs.)*

So if the cartels of crooks who get together to manufacture the stuff *(Link A of new chain #3.)* and add other materials *(A linked to B)*, and there's the whole illegality of it *(B linked to C which relates back to links in chain #2, relinking and rechaining has begun.)* which causes people to use the drugs in unhygienic and unsafe ways *(C leads to D which related back to links in chain #2, affect on human body.)*, unsupervised ways *(D leads to E)*, and there's also the fascination of something that's illegal. *(E leads to F which relates back to chain #2, illicit use.)* So you can almost see it's bound to thrive the more illegal it is. *(F leads to G, end of chain #3 regarding manufacturing, illegality and harmful effects, which also includes relinked material from chain #2.)*

What I'm leading to is that I think the drug laws are wrong; *(Link A, new position, new chain #4.)* most people in this country who die from drug-related diseases die of alcohol-related diseases *(A leads to B)*, and possibly smoking as well *(B leads to C)*, both those are legalized drugs;

(C leads to D) and we also have significant—not only deaths *(D leads to E)*, but long-term problems at work with chronic ill-health caused by smoking and alcohol. *(E leads to F, relinking of material from chains #1, #2, and #3 including effect on body of alcohol and cigarettes, as legal drugs in relation to effect on body of illicit drugs.)*

So I would say that the way to deal with the drug problem, first of all, is decriminalizing and issuing of drugs to people who really are addicted *(New position, chain #5, link A which relinks legal issue and addictive issue.)*, the prescriptive use controlled by the government would probably get rid of an awful lot of the crime *(A leads to B, legal issue in relation to community good.)* and certainly it would get rid of the health problems *(B leads to C, legal relinked with health issues.)*, and in the end these people, many of them I believe could be rehabilitated if they are addicted. *(C leads to D, desired outcome of chain #5 as a course of action.)*

I'm very much in favor of education rather than control, *(New position, chain #6, link A relates to link A, chain #5.)* but I bear in mind *(This is almost the same statement as "on the one hand-on the other hand", both indicate that the speaker is holding two chains in mind and relinking them to make his/her position/argument clear.)* that we've got a situation now where a large percentage of the population—two or three percent maybe—are uneducated in this area *(A leads to B in chain #6.)*, in that case I would want to control their lives for them a little by prescribing the stuff if they're hooked on it. *(B leads to C relates back to links A and B in chain #5.)* Education—alcohol and tobacco I think we're having a tremendous success now with banning advertising of cigarettes *(C leads to D)*, we still get far too many young people who are taking up smoking *(D leads to E)*, but I mean we have to start somewhere and I know my six-year old would never consider the concept of smoking as anything less than certain death because the advertising that's now on TV aimed at his age—very important. *(E leads to F)* Same thing with alcohol, *(F leads to G)* and hopefully the next generation that's coming along—fewer of them will be badly affected because they will have been better educated *(G leads to H)*.

Note: not one approach but the integration of multiple approaches is the essence of parallel processing. Subject D's interview is a good example of the complex relinking and rechaining that one observes in the mental processing we call bi-conditional parallel processing.

Jaques & Cason

Re-read Subject D's interview, omitting comments to get a sharper perception of the interplay and interweaving of the sequential chains.

Subject E
C1 Abstract Conceptual Or-Or Declarative Processing
Third Order Information Complexity

Here the discrete reasons for Subject E's position in the discussion of a work issue come in the form of complex paragraphs, stated in abstract conceptual terms, as compared with the much simpler statements of subject A with which it should be compared for the similarity in process. The conclusions are drawn using declarative or-or processing of third order information concepts such as requisite working relationships vs. non-trust inducing relationships vs. technical expertise. Read the interview without stopping—it gives a staccato feel, typical of C1.

Interviewer: That's how you operate? So it's not just advisory. And if I don't take it higher it means that I'm not worried about your not accepting my advice.

Subject E: Well, the problem there is that if you operate like that, you go from a chemist who's an expert in the field, you then move the thing up to the general manager, shall we say, who quite frankly is not necessarily an expert in the field either. And that's really where we stand. The general manager may say, "well, fellows," he's probably not going to admit that he doesn't understand but he's going to be reluctant to force the issue, because he's got two equal people and he doesn't want to be seen to be coming down on the side of one. *(This paragraph is a declarative statement even though it contains within it the last sentence which includes 2nd order cumulative processing. Each of us has a most complex level of mental processing beyond which we cannot work; however, we often use lesser processes in some parts of our engrossed arguments. This is a good example.)*

Interviewer: Now we come into the heart of the problem, which isn't between the chemist and the manager, it's the chemist and the general manager.

Subject E: Well not so much, it's that, if you were in a position—just shift the emphasis for a moment—if I was in a position of a manager and I had two subordinates who don't agree, I don't like the situation very much, I feel uncomfortable and they feel uncomfortable—it may worry me less than it worries other people but it certainly worries a lot of people.

Interviewer: Let's say I am your subordinate, you're general manager and here's my colleague.

Subject E: So if you two people are warring among yourselves, or just don't agree, the natural reaction is to try and find a conciliatory course of action that doesn't upset either of you. And that is what nine people out of ten will do. They won't come down hard on the side of the person who's producing the right answer, and this is human nature I think. It's certainly been my experience from previous jobs. *(A complex declarative statement about human nature.)*

But the thing that really concerns me is that we have these experts, or nominated experts, or nominated groups in the expert field in support and advisory roles, who have an enormous difficulty in influencing the main thrust of the business; and it is either because the organization per se is less than ideal or it may well be that the personalities in the organization are not the personalities you would hope to get in an ideal organization.

So that if you have a dominant person in an active role, who doesn't want to take advice from the experts, then you've got real problems; and to a very large extent I would say throughout our organization this is a major stumbling block. *(A number of conceptual or-or, disjunctive or unconnected statements, about experts, human nature, the main thrust of the business, and personality factors.)*

If I were to enjoy a very good relationship—and I do—with some of the managers here and they say, we know you're the expert and we will listen to everything you say with bated breath, and we'll do what you say and it works, that's great; but if we have somebody else that says, "I'm running my own show, thanks. I don't necessarily agree with anything that you're about to say, I may or may not do what you want," that to me seems to be crazy; because I say to my president in no uncertain terms, "If you want brain surgery, I reckon you ought to go and see a brain surgeon rather than a plumber." But here we push a lot of plumbers to the forefront and that's not sensible. *(A third complex declarative statement, about the abstract concept of a company's (de)valuing of expertise.)*

This is a major problem: We have many experts in the various disciplines, whether it's chemistry or engineering, accountancy, business analysis, whatever, but we are saying to those people, who may well be skilled, very skilled in their own disciplines, "You give the advice, we may or may not take it, and depending on how good you are at selling that advice, this will perhaps assist or mitigate against that advice being taken." Now to my way of thinking that's all crazy. *(Another complex declarative or-or statement not explicitly connected to any other.)*

Re-read Subject E's interview, omitting comments to get a sharper perception of the staccato effect of or-or, declarative processing.

These last three cases are not taken from our study since the problems of providing anonymity were too difficult to overcome. The views of people at these levels can be readily recognizable to others who know them. Here the arguments build up cumulatively. The and-ands build up in relation to each other, giving a more reflective quality.

Subject F (Not a participant in the study.)
C2 Abstract Conceptual And-And Cumulative Processing
Third Order Information Complexity

Subject F: Well, what about world politics? My view is that politics generally come back to a law. People adopt extreme positions, and ultimately those extreme positions are shown to fail, and people get back to the law. If you look at great political upheavals in the world—what happened in the First World War and the Second World War, the two major upheavals that have occurred this century? You find that those were really based on ignorance and the way people were led to think by their leaders. And if they had thought through where they were going logically, they would never have adopted the positions that they took in those conflicts. *(Statement of position or point of view using cumulatively connected concepts of the law and politics and world upheavals and ignorance.)*

Interviewer: In whose sense—what do you mean by logically?

Subject F: Logically if they had thought through where this path was ultimately going to take them. If you took the Japanese, for instance, in 1940-41, if they had thought through where an attack on Pearl Harbor was going to take them, I doubt very much whether they would ever have attacked Pearl Harbor. *(Declarative paragraph giving position or conclusion Subject F will argue for.)*

Interviewer: Are you suggesting that they didn't think it through?

Subject F: I think they thought it through only in the short-term way. They had a problem insofar as they thought they were being surrounded by a white European power <u>and</u> they had to break out of that, <u>and</u> the way they did that they thought was to enter armed conflict, which in the long run turned out to be a failure. The point I was trying to get to was that in politics extreme positions are taken really by keeping the population ignorant of many facts, <u>and</u> you can only take people to do extreme things if they only see one part of the story. *(Several connected and-and reasons using the concept of the nature of political actions taken by populations with controlled access to information.)* <u>And</u> I think if they see the full story they tend to adopt more moderate and center-of-the-road attitudes; <u>and</u> the real thing that's happening in world politics today, I think, is that people have greater access to information, have greater access to different opinions. You can't keep them ignorant, <u>and</u> so therefore they tend to want to gravitate to a more mean position. *(More and-and connections.)*

And this is what's been happening in the Eastern bloc countries. With the advent of television <u>and</u> satellite television it's very difficult to jam, people have access to that information, <u>and</u> because of that they want to share in the fruits of—not a democratic system, because that's too trite—it's very difficult to define, but in a life where they have a greater say in their future, greater say in how they're going to be governed, and greater opportunity to share in the fruits of their government. <u>And</u> their force is so irresistible. Even if you think through history <u>and</u> if you say what if the world turned their back on Adolf Hitler <u>and</u> said OK, Adolf, "You go and do your own thing." <u>And</u> if Britain didn't serve an ultimatum in 1939, <u>and</u> the German people did invade all of Europe <u>and</u> ultimately Britain, I wonder if the world would be much more different today than it is now. *(Another succession of supporting and-and statements about the nature of a democratic system.)*

What I think does happen is that you have blips in history, but ultimately extreme positions come back to a more mean position; people get bored with the mean position <u>and</u> then go off into extreme positions again. I think that the world has gone through a great change because, for the first time ever, the whole world can hear about the same thing almost at the same time. That means that access to information means better decisions are made, more logical decisions are made, and really the whole world comes to the same conclusion on many issues *(More and-and reasons)*.

Jaques & Cason

Re-read Subject F's interview, omitting comments to get a sharper perception of the and-and, cumulative processing.

Note: throughout this interview Subject F has dealt with concepts of law and information and their impact on people's choices, making the argument for this point of view by accumulating reasons. The and-and reasoning builds up continuously and cumulatively. But the reasons are not organized into explicitly chained sequential links. That particular processing is presented below by Subject G.

Subject G *(Not a participant in the study.)*
C3 Abstract Conceptual If-Then-Then Serial Processing
Third Order Information Complexity

Here, as in B3, the flow of the argument is strongly serial if-then chains, but the information used is abstract conceptual.

Interviewer: What about legalization of drugs?

Subject G: Having two teenage children, it's obviously an issue that one thinks about and talks about, talks with the kids about. I guess where I am on that issue at the moment, (thankfully the kids are all heavily into sports so they're non-drinkers, non-smokers, non-drug-takers; but they do see it in the schools, they've been through good schools, so I'm well out of it. They know about it; they've been offered drugs, and say, and I believe, that they've rejected them. I guess that gives me the ability to take a somewhat disinterested but at the same time interested view.

I must say that the theory of legalization I find very attractive, because clearly for whatever reason we're not winning the war against illicit or illegal drugs *(Chain #1, link A.)*; and I can certainly accept the economic thesis that says, because they're illegal they command a higher value *(Link B)* and it's the higher value that encourages relatively immature children, young adults, particularly. People with problems I think are in a different category—the defiance-of-authority syndrome—the illicit statement, I think has a lot to do with many kids starting down the path. *(Link C)* So I find very attractive the position for children to try the defiance of authority thing and the excitement of doing something illicit. *(Re-statement of link C.)* And if they're not illegal and can be obtained at nominal cost, then you take the economic drive out of the supply side of the equation. *(Link D. Concepts of illicit drugs, economic thesis, defiance of authority syndrome, economic drive, supply side chained together in an if-then relationship of if A then B, if B then C, if C then D.)*

I have a fundamental revulsion to legalization, but I have to say I think if I were faced with voting on a decision, I'd probably come down on the side of legalization *(Chain #2, link A.)*, provided the transition arrangements were sensible and provided some control *(Link B)*, because frankly I despair of our society's winning the war against illegal drugs. *(Link C. Chain #2 is created with links A, B, and C.)*

I think one of the most stunning victories for social persuasion, one of the most outstanding examples of social change conceived in the last twenty years has been the anti-smoking thing—absolutely extraordinary. *(Chain #3, link A.)* There you have legal supply *(Link B)*, and by subtly using existing advertising and other techniques to change social perceptions, we've been able to make a spectacular difference to people's use of tobacco. *(Link C)* Total tobacco consumption hasn't fallen. *(Link D)* I believe that's because we continue to allow the promotion of tobacco as something attractive and in some ways again give it an almost forbidden-fruit type of image to kids. *(Link E. Chain #3 is created with links A, B, C, D, E.)*

So I'm an advocate of the ban on advertising of tobacco. *(Chain #4, link A.)* By all means, have cigarettes available in the shops at a price, but ban promotion. *(Link B)* They're there if people want them but they're not encouraged *(Link C)*, and continue the promotion of anti-social aspects of smoking. *(Link D. But Subject G does not explicitly link the tobacco theme back to the drugs as would be expected in parallel processing which is demonstrated by Subject H below.)*

Re-read Subject G's interview, omitting comments to note more clearly the sequential or serial pattern.

Subject H *(Not a participant in the study.)*
C4 Abstract Conceptual If-and-Only-If Parallel Processing
Third Order Information Complexity

In this material, there is substantial cross-relating of the links in several if-then serial chains creating new chains of if-and-only-if chains using abstract concepts.

Subject H: Let's take the subject I've spent a little more time thinking about, legalization of drugs. My background was that I did a little work in getting a rehabilitation program established here. A lot of us went out and door knocked and raised money and got government support. *(Chain #1, history.)*

The drug thing does worry me. At the present moment I think I probably am in favor of legalization because at the present moment I see us on a highway to nothing. If you legalize it, in my judgment you probably will have more addicts and there will probably be more deaths as a result of legalizing it, caused by drugs, than would be the truth now. So if there are two percent addicts now and if there are six percent who tried, you might finish up with three percent addicts and 10 percent that tried. So we have to realize that legalizing it probably increases the use of it: this on balance I think is a worry. *(Chain #2, link A—legalization, link B—leading to more addicts, link C—leading to a worrying problem.)*

Offsetting that I think you would have the opportunity then to use publicity to say to people, "It's not a big thing to try and get your kicks that way," and therefore over time I don't think that's a permanent problem *(Chain #3, link A.)*, but the reason why I'm worried at the present moment is that the sheer financial benefits from people peddling drugs and the cost to people of getting the money to pay for the habit, seem to me to be cutting across all our systems of government, our police, etc., etc. *(A leads to B)*, so I'm not certain that the community isn't suffering worse damage out of people having to get their drugs and get it in a way that is destructive to society *(B leads to C)*.

So on balance *(Chain #4)* I'm worried that prohibition years ago created the gangsters *(A leads to B)*, and I'm a bit inclined to think that the drug systems are creating the same sort of problem today *(B leads to C)* and that you'd be better to legalize it even though the results would be *(C leads to D)* a number of people more killed by drugs than would otherwise be the case. *(This chain deals with prohibition, financial benefits to sellers, costs to buyers, community damages, history, gangsters, drug deaths.)*

Interviewer: But aren't people killed by alcohol?

Subject H: I agree, drugs are a much more addictive thing. And if I didn't think that we are now past the point of no return in stopping it—therefore, I think you're better to legalize it and not criminalize it *(Chain #5 relinking chain #2, link A to chain #3, link B/C.)* and create the circumstances in which there isn't money for people to peddle it. *(Another link to chain #3, link A.)* There are going to be mass-produced scientifically developed drugs which will do a lot of damage. *(Another link in chain #5.)* But they're sufficiently rampant now, I don't think you'd stop everybody by doing it any other way *(Another link to chain #2.)*, so on balance I think it's very much the lesser of two evils. *(Last link in chain #5, a rechained argument.)*

If you say to me, what are you doing, I'm saying to you that my way of viewing things which are difficult like this is to say there is an extreme. *(Chain #6, link A.)* If there is one-hundredth of one percent chance and by throwing the law book you could stop it, then that's a different matter. *(A leads to B)* We are now in a situation where you can idealize how you could have stopped it, but you can't, totally *(B leads to C)*, not saying it's a sin and a bad thing, I think is wrong *(Link D)*, so what I think is there is a choice to be made among the balance of nasties in which I think not legalizing gives us a slightly worse set of circumstances for the whole society it being illegal, than would be if it was legal. *(Relates this link back to chains #2, 3, 4 and 5.)*

Interviewer: So you're talking about the possibility of a marginal gain, but no big deal.

Subject H: No, no—I think the pressure on corruption of the police and the judiciary and society as a whole through the amount of money in drugs is more than a marginal impact on society. So that if you think of Chicago in the 1930s, it was more than just marginally damaging and this is subverting the government and the whole structure. *(This last argument is a rechaining of the previous concepts and information given in earlier chains.)*

The information used throughout is strongly abstract conceptual—such as systems of government, the police and the judiciary, idealization, society-as-a-whole.

Re-read Subject H's interview, omitting comments to get a sharper perception of the interplay and interweaving of the sequential chains.

It has been our intention in this appendix to demonstrate how the four mental processes and the orders of information complexity are manifested in adults working to support a particular position regarding a subject of interest. These annotated interviews are samples of the ordinary, everyday discourse we all encounter as we interact at work, socially and in family life.

A First Formulation of
Discontinuity—1964

The following document was prepared by Jaques in 1964 for the general manager of Manufacturing at the Glacier Metal Company as part of the Glacier Project. It was a first attempt at an hypothesis that might explain the natural managerial layers that had been found in the late 1950s. Glacier had already implemented that structure, and the general manager was keen to develop a better understanding of what they were doing. It will be noted that he used a concept of levels of abstracting, and that he did not have a clear understanding of the fact that he was compressing both complexity of work in role and complexity of mental processing into the same hypothesis. This hypothesis, along with several others along the way, was shown to be incorrect, and was rejected. But it was a start, and contained some seeds for the eventual growth of our current ideas.

11th February, 1964

To: Sir John Paget.
From: Social Science Officer.

<u>LEVELS OF ABSTRACTION</u>

<u>Rank-1 level of abstraction</u>: The individual
needs to have his work physically present in order
to work on it. He cannot do work away from it.

<u>Rank-2 level of abstraction</u>: He can work with
an imaginal picture of a physical thing.

<u>Rank-3 level of abstraction</u>: He can construct
an imaginal picture from a conceptual description
- for example, from load data about future load.

<u>Rank-4 level of abstraction</u>: He can start with
an image of the physical task, detach himself from
it, and resolve problems or prepare plans by
conceptualising the problem, and then re-state the
whole thing in concrete terms.

<u>Rank-5 level of abstraction</u>: He can cope with
practical situations by the interaction of theories
- explicit or implicit - plus "one-time contact
with the concrete", i.e., can work with a theory
illustrated by only one example.

<u>Rank-6 and Rank-7</u> levels of abstraction remain
unformulated.

Representation of memo sent by Jaques to the general manager of
manufacturing at the Glacier Metal Company, detailing Jaques'
first formulation of discontinuity in the natural managerial layers
he had discerned in the late 1950s.

Jaques & Cason

Glossary for Human Capability

This glossary sets out the definitions of the new concepts developed for the Human Capability studies, which have been added to the long list of concepts previously developed and defined from Dr. Jaques' earlier books: *Time-Span Handbook, Levels of Abstraction, A General Theory of Bureaucracy, The Form of Time, Requisite Organization* and *Executive Leadership*.

Accountability — a situation where an individual can be called to account for his/her actions by another individual or body authorized both to do so and to give recognition to the individual for those actions. See managerial accountability.

Authority — the power vested in a person by virtue of role to expend resources: financial, material, technical and human.

Bi-Conditional — a relationship in logic in which q can occur *if-and-only-if* p occurs.

Capability — the ability of a person to do work.

Coaching — regular discussions between a manager and an immediate subordinate in which the manager helps the subordinate to increase his/her skilled knowledge so that the subordinate is able to handle an increasing amount of the full range of work available in the subordinate's role.

Complexity — determined by the number of factors, the rate of change of those factors and the ease of identification of the factors in a situation.

Complexity of Mental Processing (CMP) — the complexity of mental activity a person uses in carrying out work. There are four types of mental processing.

Conditional — a relationship in logic in which *if* p occurs *then* q will occur.

Current Applied Capability (CAC) — the capability someone has to do a certain kind of work in a specific role at a given level at the present time. It is a function of his/her complexity of mental processing (CMP), how much s/he values the work of the role (V), his/her skilled use of knowledge for the tasks in the role (K/S), and the absence of pathological temperamental characteristics (minus T). We can think of this as CAC=ƒ CMP • V• K/S • (-T)

Current Potential Capability (CPC) — a person's highest current level of mental complexity. It determines the maximum level at which someone could work at the present time, given the opportunity to do so and provided that the work is of value to him/her, and given the opportunity to acquire the necessary skilled knowledge. This is the level of work that people aspire to have and feel satisfied if they can get. When people have work at their CPC, they feel they have an opportunity for the full expression of their potential.

Decision — the making of a choice with the commitment of resources.

Equilibration — the balancing by managers of the standards being used by their immediate subordinate managers in appraising and directing their own immediate subordinates.

Equitable Pay Differentials — differences in payment between work at different levels that are experienced by the incumbents as fair and just.

Future Potential Capability (FPC) — the maximum level at which a person will be capable of working at some time in the future, say at 5, 10, or 15 years from now.

Gearing (for talent pool) — the process whereby the MoR and immediate subordinate managers check their judgments with each other regarding the levels of current potential capability of individuals in the next two layers down.

Knowledge (K) — consists of facts, including procedures, that have been articulated and can be reproduced.

Level of Work (LoW) in Role — the weight of responsibility felt in roles as a result of the complexity of the work in the role. The level of work in any role can be measured by the time-span of discretion of the tasks in that role.

Manager — a person in a role which carries managerial accountability and authority.

Managerial Accountability — the accountability managers have for their own personal effectiveness; the output of their subordinates; exercising effective managerial leadership of their subordinates; building and sustaining an effective team of subordinates.

Managerial Authority — the power vested in a person by virtue of role to expend resources: financial, material, technical and human

Managerial Hierarchies — organizations used for employing people to get work done. They are employment systems organized into accountability hierarchies of manager and subordinate roles.

Manager-once-Removed (MoR) — the manager of a subordinate's immediate manager is that subordinate's manager-once-removed.

Maturation — a process in which a given aspect of a person is biologically innate and grows in a regular way to a predictable end state, so long as the individual does not encounter any severely limiting environmental conditions, especially in infancy.

Measurement — the quantification of a property of an entity by means of an objective measuring instrument.

Mental Mode — the highest level of mental processing to which an individual will finally mature.

Mental Processing — the use of a particular mental process for handling information in order to do work. The four methods of processing information are: Declarative; Cumulative; Serial; Parallel.

Mentoring — a periodic discussion by a manager-once-removed (MoR) to help a subordinate-once-removed (SoR) to understand his/her potential and how that potential might be developed to achieve as full a career growth in the organization as possible.

Order of Information Complexity — the four types of mental processing have been found to recur at higher and higher orders of complexity of the information that is being processed, giving a recursive hierarchy of levels of mental complexity.

Organizational Structure — a system of role relationships—of positions people hold in working together that establish the boundaries within which people relate to each other.

Requisite Organization — the pattern of connections which ought to exist between roles if the system is to work efficiently and to operate as required by the nature of the work to be done and the nature of human nature.

Role — a position within an organization.

Role Complexity — the complexity in a role as measured by time-span.

Role Relationships — connections between roles in a social system that define working relationships between individuals who occupy those roles in terms of accountability, authority and content.

Skill (S) — an ability, learned through experience and practice, to carry out a given procedure without having to pay attention, i.e. what a person has learned to do without thinking through the steps involved.

Social System — a network of roles and role relationships.

Stratum (plural Strata) — organizational layers in a managerial hierarchy. The work in a given stratum is characterized by a specific range of complexity.

Subordinate-once-Removed (SoR) — the subordinate of a manager's immediate subordinate is that manager's subordinate-once-removed.

Talent Pool Development (TPD) — a system for the development of a population of employees who have a distribution of current and future potential capability to discharge the company's current and future human resourcing requirements. The system includes talent pool mapping, selection, recruitment, mentoring, lateral transfers and other methods of individual career development.

Task — an assignment to produce a specified output. The specifications include Quantity (Q) and Quality (Q), a targeted completion Time (T), allocated Resources (R) and within prescribed limits of policies,

Task *(continued)*
> procedures, rules and regulations. A task is a "what by when" or a QQT/R.

Task Complexity — the complexity of information that has to be handled in carrying out a task. No measure of task complexity has yet been developed.

Temperament (T) — the tendency a person has to behave in given ways. Temperament gives the emotional color to personal interactions. Minus T (-T) refers to temperamental qualities in an individual that are dysfunctional in the sense of preventing that individual from carrying out the work required.

Time-Horizon — a method of quantifying an individual's potential capability, in terms of the longest time-span s/he could handle at a given point in their maturation process.

Time-Span of Discretion (T/S) — the targeted completion time of the longest task or task sequence in a role. Time-span measures level of work in a role.

Values (V) — those things to which an individual will give priority or wants to do. Values are vectors which direct our actions.

Work — the exercise of judgment and discretion in making decisions in carrying out goal directed activities.

Bibliography

Anstey, E. (1977) "A Thirty Year Follow-Up of the CSSB Procedure, with Lessons for the Future," *Journal of Occupational Psychology*, 50, 149-159.

Bion, Wilfred R. (1962) "Learning from Experience" H. Karnac Books, Ltd., London.

Boals, David (1992) "The 'Information Age' as an Un-Informing Social Ideology," *Elliott Jaques Festschrift*, Cason Hall, Falls Church, VA.

Bray, D. W. and A. Howard (1983) "The AT&T Longitudinal Studies of Managers," in K. W. Schail (Ed) *Longitudinal Studies of Adult Psychological Development*, 266-312, Guilford Press, New York, NY.

Bruner, Jerome (1966) *Toward a Theory of Instruction,* Norton & Co., New York, NY.

Bucy, Flynn (1988) "A Typology of Reasoning Based on Elliott Jaques' Quintave Model of Cognitive Functioning Applied to Moral Problem Solving," *Doctoral Dissertation*, George Washington University, Washington, D.C.

Cole, M. and S. Cole (1993) *The Development of Children,* Scientific American Books, New York, NY.

Commons, M.J., F.A. Richards, and C. Armon, Eds. (1984) *Beyond Formal Operations,* Prager, New York, NY.

Fischer, K.W. (1980) "How Cognitive Processes and Environmental Conditions Organize Discontinuities in the Development of Abstractions," in C. Alexander and E. Lauger, *Higher Stages in Human Development*, Oxford University Press, New York, NY.

(1989) "A Theory of Cognitive Development," *Psychological Review*, Vol. 87, 477-531.

Gibson, R.O. and D.J. Isaac (1978) "Truth Tables as a Formal Device in the Analysis of Human Actions," in Jaques, Gibson, and Isaac, *Levels of Abstraction in Logic and Human Action*, Cason Hall, Falls Church, VA.

Homa, Edna (1967) "The Inter-Relationship Among Work, Payment and Capacity," *Doctoral Dissertation*, Harvard Business School, Cambridge, MA.

Hunter, J.E. and R.F (1984) "Validity and Utility of Alternative Predictors of Performance," *Psychological Bulletin*, 96, 72-98.

Isaac, John and B. O'Connor (1978) "A Discontinuity Theory of Psychological Development," in Jaques, Gibson, and Isaac, *Levels of Abstraction in Logic and Human Action*, Cason Hall, Falls Church, VA.

Jaques, Elliott

(1956) *Measurement of Responsibility*, Cason Hall, Falls Church, VA.

(1964) *Time-Span Handbook*, Cason Hall, Falls Church, VA.

(1961) *Equitable Payment*, Cason Hall, Falls Church, VA.

(1965) "Preliminary Sketch of a General Structure of Executive Strata," Brown, W. and Jaques, *Glacier Project Papers*, Cason Hall, Falls Church, VA.

(1976) *A General Theory of Bureaucracy*, reprinted (1993) Gregg Revivals, London.

(1978) *Levels of Abstraction in Logic and Human Action*, Cason Hall, Falls Church, VA.

(1982) *Free Enterprise, Fair Employment*, Cason Hall, Falls Church, VA.

(1982) *The Form of Time*, Cason Hall, Falls Church, VA.

(1986) "The Development of Intellectual Capability," *Journal of Applied Behavioral Science*, 22, 361-383.

(1989) *Requisite Organization*, Cason Hall, Falls Church, VA, also distributed by Gower, London.

(1990) "Learning for Uncertainty," *Creativity and Work*, International Universities Press, Inc., Madison, CT.

(1991) with Clement, S. *Executive Leadership*, Cason Hall, Falls Church, VA, and Basil Blackwell, Oxford.

Klein, Melanie (1975) *Narrative of a Child Analysis, Collected Writings, The Psychoanalysis of Children*, Hogarth Press, London.

Kohler, T. (1986) Unpublished analysis of follow-up data collected by Jaques.

Kegan, R. (1982) *The Emerging Self*, Harvard University Press, Cambridge, MA.

Levinson, Daniel (1978) *The Seasons of a Man's Life*, Knopf Publishing Group, New York, NY.

Macdonald, Ian (1978) "Five Levels of Mental Handicap," in *Levels of Abstraction in Logic and Human Action*, Cason Hall, Falls Church, VA.

Piaget, Jean (1952) *The Origins of Intelligence in Children*, International Universities Press, Stamford, CT.

(1957) *Logic and Psychology*, Basic Books, New York, NY.

(1977) *The Development of Thought*, Viking, New York, NY.

Richardson, Roy (1971) *Fair Pay and Work*, Heinemann Educational Books Ltd., London.

Spearman, C. (1927) *The Abilities of Man*, Macmillan, New York, NY.

Stamp, Gillian (1988) "Longitudinal Research into Methods of Assessing Managerial Potential," *Technical Report 819*, US Army Research Institute for Behavioral and Social Sciences, Alexandria, VA.

Vernon, P.A. (1990) "An Overview of Chronometric Measures of Intelligence," *School Psychology Review*, 4, 399-410.

Zuckerkandl, Viktor (1956) *Sound and Symbol: Music and the External World*, Tr. by Willard R. Trask, Pantheon Books Inc., Bollingen Series, New York, NY.

Index